New
and
Selected
Poems

My vines are vines; each tangible full rondure
Is just itself, no symbol and no dream.
That dust is three-dimensional. The olives
Are really there. I am the land I seem.
— "Etruria," p. 79

Poetry by Peter Viereck

The First Morning: Lyrical Poems
The Persimmon Tree: Pastoral Poems
Strike Through the Mask
Terror and Decorum
The Tree Witch

Peter Viereck

New and Selected Poems 1932-1967

THE BOBBS-MERRILL COMPANY, INC.
A Subsidiary of Howard W. Sams & Co., Inc.
Publishers Indianapolis New York Kansas City

For the poet Alexis Viereck

A sketch of the coast at Rockport, Mass., by Philippine-born painter Fernando Zóbel illustrating "Walks on the Edge," Chapter 10.

Prefatory Note

The earliest poems are "Dies Illa" and "A Walk on Snow" (1932–33). The latest are the "Snow Against Rain" and the concluding "Walks on the Edge" (1966–67). When a book encapsules more than 30 of the author's 50 years, perhaps a line gets drawn.

Lest a clutter of chronology distract from the verse itself, most dates have been added only for the very early poems (before 1947) and the very recent ones (after 1961, the time of the last book). Except for a few poems completed long before publication, dates have been omitted for poems published during 1948–61, as all such poems are in the author's five previous verse books, already dated: *Terror and Decorum*, 1948; *Strike Through the Mask*, 1950; *The First Morning*, 1952; *The Persimmon Tree*, 1956; *The Tree Witch*, 1961.*

The ten chapters are arranged not chronologically but by topic. Often a poem is so placed as to extend or modify the preceding poem. Thereby the basic unit of the book becomes, in part, the progression not of the poem but of the chapter.

---

* All published by Charles Scribner's Sons, in hardcover editions. All five are out of print (with copyright reversion to the author) except for the few remaining copies of *The First Morning*. Acknowledgment to Scribner's is herewith gratefully rendered, with recollections of pleasant associations.

The author's most representative poem in form and content (representative, not favorite or best) is probably the one called "Autumn Instant" in earlier books (here split, in a stage version, into the two untitled songs of pages 143–144). Since poems speak for themselves, there is no obligation to preface a poetry book with a literary credo; in one of his prose books (the "Dignity of Lyricism" chapter of *The Unadjusted Man* in its 1962 paperback version) the author did make a try at such a credo; it will have to suffice.

Some 20 new poems have been included (either entirely new or basically rewritten). Their post-1961 dates are appended to indicate their not having appeared before in book form. From the five previous verse books, the author has selected perhaps 20 percent for reprinting here (often slightly revised).

Except for the new poems, the cumbersome apparatus of acknowledgment of prior magazine publication may be dispensed with in a book of almost 100 poems; in the case of the old poems, the copyright-maintaining acknowledgments to magazines have already been made in the prior books. Yet the author does owe a more personal acknowledgment to the four magazines that, right from the beginning, published his poems most often (in the sense of six or more): *Poetry, Harper's, Botteghe Oscure,* and John Crowe Ransom's *Kenyon Review* of the 1940's. And where the poems were rejected by magazines or critics, the resultant self-criticism and revision often proved equally helpful to these pages.

PETER VIERECK
South Hadley, Mass.

January, 1967

Foreword: Walks and Trees
(for chapters 10 and 1)

. . . and boyhoods, long green afternoons.
Then actions, handcuffs of an inward tune.
Walks are the middle jungle. Walks on whom?
>   To walk around inside our unmapped own
>   Skin is what makes these ambles fumble so
>   Purposeful. What else is their momentum
>   But immobility?—a cramped sequoia's
>   Propulsive tiredness, a rage to surge
>   Beyond the furthest resin upwardness.
And who—speak, skeleton—inside his skin
Is not a walker, not a walking tree?

1967

Acknowledgments

Poems not previously published in book form:

"The Two Again," *Prairie Schooner*, 1967
"Grace of Pine," *Tri-Quarterly*, 1965
"Dance of the Haemophiliacs," *Tri-Quarterly*, 1966
"The Entropy Song" and "Counterwalk," *Tri-Quarterly*, 1967
"Ode to Joy," *Antioch Review*, 1967
"An Owl for a Nightingale," *Whetstone*, 1967
"The Lyricism of the Weak," *Prairie Schooner*, 1965
"River," *Minnesota Review*, 1964
"Ode," "Paean," and "Threnode," *Minnesota Review*, 1965
"Steps to the Sea," "A Wreath for a Plunge," and "More Than Wings Can Bear," *Massachusetts Review*, 1966
"Killed by a Car," *Christian Century*, 1967
"The New Cultural Blues," *Florida Quarterly*, 1967
"Fiftieth Birthday," *New York Times*, 1967

The poems from the five earlier titles (out of print) are already copyrighted by the author with over 100 magazine acknowledgments therein noted. These copyrights are herewith reaffirmed. See Prefatory Note for dates and titles of the five books.

Contents

1: The Tree Menagerie

2: The Girl Menagerie

3 : Earth

4 : Sky

5 : Wars

6 : Persimmons

7 : Cradle Songs and Elegies

8: Grotesques

9: Two Scenes from a Play

10 : Walks

1: The Tree Menagerie

"An inward-facing mask is what must break."
—page 97

I Alone Am Moving

(an adolescent sapling addresses humanity)

You all are static; I alone am moving.
Racing beyond each planted Pullman wheel,
      I pity you and long to reel
You through my thousand outstretched ways of loving.
Are you alive at all? Can non-trees feel?

Run while I may, for at my pith gnaws night.
The winds—these are great stacks of anchored air;
      I thresh them with my hard-pronged hair;
I jump right through them, roaring my delight.
Live while I may—run, run, no matter where.

How marvelous, if you but knew, is speed!
You all must wait; I am your overtaker.
      Striding to green from yellow acre,
I toss you spring. Each dawn, my tendrils knead
Stars into pancake-suns like a tall baker.

Trudging toward snowtime, I can mope for hours
To think of birds, the birds I leave behind.
      Why did the God who keeps you blind,
Instead give sight and sentience to my flowers?
Black questions in my sap outwear my rind.

Humans (I almost envy you your peace)
Are free of this gnarled urge for Absolutes
      Which sweetens and saddens all my fruits,
Dragging my twigs down when I'd fly towards bliss—
While bugs and diamonds agonize my roots.

The Slacker Apologizes

"An artist is a philistine despite himself, a patriotic moralist with a bad conscience. When his art shouts 'beauty,' his conscience shouts 'duty!' Solution unsatisfactory."

—The Manndelbaum Chronicles

We trees were chopping down the monsters in the
    Street to count their rings.
WHO BLEST OUR WAR? The oak invoked: "Within Thee
Crush, Mother, quakingly these red-sapped things
    Whose harrowings
Wrong Thy clean dirt. Kill, kill all alien kings."

Crowned by black moss or by obscener yellow,
    The flowerless monsters stood
On soil-blaspheming asphalt. How they'd bellow
Each time we hacked them—just as if their crude
    Numb root-pairs could
Feel feeling. O Goddess, the glory of being wood!

Then games of peace. WHO WAS THE POET? I!
    I was the willow lyre.
Even the oak was silent; melody
Maddened whole meadows like a forest-fire
    To hear my choir
Of leaves beat, beat, and beat upon each wire

Of winds I tamed and tuned so artfully
    It seemed an artless game.
You! weed back there!, don't think I didn't see
You yawning. Bored? Well, try to do the same!
    What? Suddenly lame?
Come, come, step up and sing—or wither in shame.

Then crooned the crass young weed: *"Last night my stamen*
    Could hear her pistil sigh.

4

Though far the garden that her petals flame in,
We touched in dreams the hour that bee flew by.
      My pollen's shy
Deep nuzzling tells her: weeds must love or die."

Fools. How they cheered. But wait, I set them right:
      "Verse, verse, not poetry.
Jingles for jungles: grosser groves delight
In honey; but educated tastes decree
      Austerity.
True art is bitter, but true art sets free.

"True art, how can I serve thee half enough?
      Had I a thousand sprays
And every spray a thousand sprigs, they'd sough
For beauty, beauty, beauty all their days—
      And still not praise
Not half the whirlwind-wonder of thy ways."

At this the oak, our captain, roared me down:
      "Mere beauty wilts the will.
Why are we here? To sing and play the clown?"
The forest answered: "We are here to kill."
      . . . While monsters still
Defile Thy loam, while trees know right from wrong,

Forgive me, Mother, for the guilt of song.

The Slacker Need Not Apologize

"The core has its resins of which the resin knows nothing."
                                        —PASCAL

ACT I

(oak to willow)

It's I, your gnarled accuser, here to scold.
What REALLY do you know of earth and sky?
Which different raindrops can you classify?

How many kinds of dung identify?
From too much staring at the shapes of winds,
You're blinder than a stump to honest mold,
Gall, mildew, all true tree-reality.
Mad bird-cursed shaker of obstreperous crest,
Listening as if to song yet bare of nest,
Roost only of mist from whom all wings take wing:
Even our God, the weather, you deny;
You blossom when you feel like blossoming,
In a blasphemingly eternal spring.
We have a word for such un-treelike stunts.
We call them SABOTAGE. Since well-meant hints
Have failed, permit the frankness of the old;
      The grove agrees it's time you're told:
Your chance of passing next week's Woodlore Test
      Is—bear it oakly—not the best.
You know the price! The beaver-foreman claims
He needs just one more trunk to mend his dams.

ACT II

(*willow to oak*)

Mad? No, I'm madness maddened
                      (—into truth?).
When groves are mute, when outward wings are south,
Hear—can't you hear?—the humming in my sap,
Cascades more lyrical than any lark.
Your "test"? The holy winds—for love of me
Whose blindness dreams them into visibility—
      Will test your trunk with choice typhoons;
They'll stretch you with a little thunderclap
Before the foreman's tedious cuspid zeal.

(*thunder offstage; willow solo*)

The winds are but the moods we willows feel.
Our weepings are the velvet bells they peal.
Their rage and fondlings vibrate through our bark:—

From outside through?,

From inside through?,

are we

The strummers or the echoes of earth's tunes?

ACT III

(spotlight on willow's soliloquy; in background beavers in over-alls drag away storm-felled oak; stage floor as planetary globe; arched leaf overhead as sky)

Alone less sure of answers than at war.
Mere echo (—strummer?), mad (—or wild with truth?),
By contours of the winds lured far too far,
I'm left behind when even God flies south
(If "God" means all the climate I ignore).
Alone with hints of hints. The world's a burr
I'm stuck to. Dropping. Quick, grow meanings back.
Back, back; drop upward. Certainty's a rock
Too lichen-slippery for a root's attack.
There's one blue leaf: big mask;—it mocks, but I'll
Know answers when it falls; can wait. Meanwhile,
To show mere sky I'm not its servitor,
I'm burnt by snow and drunk on drouth
And serve the inner weather of my core.

My Gentlest Song

(pine to rose)

I.

Small friend, you fed my awe when I was small,
I who have never fed on soil alone.
Because I must be lit by more than sun,

7

I bless the bloom of which you'll now be shorn,
Sweetness no cone of mine can ever grow.
Your nectar wounds me wilder than your thorn;
I've loved you fresher than my youngest bud
And longer than your oldest can recall;
Yet must not help you, even if I could,
For it's not I who made you mortal. Mourn
That we—once planted by the selfsame strewing,
⠀⠀⠀⠀Pale seed by seed together flying,
You not yet rose, I not yet pine, upborne
By the same gusty randomness—must blow
Apart forever by the law of snow.

2.

Remember, friend, your dancing-days of May
When restless willows rustled just for you?
You tossed your petals such a reckless way
You hardly noticed me the whole month through
And thought your beauty was its own defense.
Yet all the while my boughs were shielding you.
You know the zephyrs, I the hurricanes;
I've suffered hail so you could sip the dew.
Because I've died so many times each fall,
Now something in me can not die at all.
But each new ring of wisdom cost me dear
In chills you'll never feel who last a year.
Now go—goodbye—while I grow still more tall;
⠀⠀⠀⠀You bore me when you look so glum;
For there's one shade I must not shade you from.

3.

Small friend, you'll never leave me any more
Though you have death and I have sleep ahead.
My beautiful hunger waits for you, it waits
To twine us ever closer than before
(Before we sprouted toward such different fates),
Close as the hour we lay there, spore by spore,

8

Two seeming twins in selfsame garden-bed.
How many times I've wished me dead instead!
How gladly I'd divide my unspent sheen
And lend your fadings half my evergreen!
But must not help you, even if I could,
For it's not I who made you less than wood.
      You—bright brief putrefying weed—
      Will feed my roots next spring, will feed
The fabulous white-hot darkness at my core.

To My Playmate, with Thanks for Carefree Days Together

1.

You are my winter-comfort, loyal fruit
That never tumbles from this hempen twig.
My flowers, for all their sun-time vows, elope
With the first snowflake; green frays off so quick;
But (faithful to the sacrament of rope
That married blood and wood) you still remain
To dance me Mayward and unfrost my hope.
When too much longing droops me with the pain
Of too much beauty; when O once again
Caress of bugs—or diamonds?—stabs my root;
When doubt, and doubt of doubt, make sap congeal:
Then I'll just twitch my branch and you'll dispel
All spells by rattling me some joyous jig.

2.

How glad-with-life you hop and swing and dangle!
Better to ride on wind than trudge on rock.
A nuzzling breeze rubs, purring, past your ankle;

Kind humble crawlers—once they feared your plow—
Now hiss affectionately from your throat;
Between your ribs a heart—a wren's—is hot.
All tears you ever lost, rain cries them back
Into your sockets. Gongs of starlight spangle
Your tar * with tintinnabulating dew—
Till black and gold and music fuse for you,
In liquid loud mosaics round your brow.

3.

What prose and platitude and meanness clogged
Your head before the black ones pecked it pure!
Next, worms and weather scrubbed the nerve-webbed mesh
Of ego out. This was a filthy chore.
Now you're a hive for honeybees. They flocked
To sweeten and to resurrect your skull.
Today it hums with dreams more beautiful
Than tuneless lusts that stung your brain before.
How long, O fruit, since ripeness burst your skin?
Commemorate that second birth. You bore
What every triviality of flesh
Is pregnant with: the perfect bone within.

Saga

(pre-Columbian runic rhythms)

1.

You must walk the plank.
I can guess why you're not in a hurry.
(*You must walk the plank.*)

* To preserve the hanged criminal (as object lesson) as long as possible from the inclemency of the elements, he was customarily painted with a protective covering of black tar.

While you walk, I'll creak you my story
    —(*You must walk the plank*)—
Of my rise from old wood to new glory.
        (*You must walk the plank.*)
You will hear only me till the hop.
        (*You must walk the plank.*)
Take pride in my rise as you drop.

2.

        Vinland the Good!
I grew old, I grew big by her sea.
        Vikings came.
Honor they brought to me.
        From all the grove
I was chosen as gallows-tree.
        Years flew by,
More swift than the crows on my fruit,
        Till the year I screamed
With the doom of an axe at my root.

3.

        Thankless thanes.
I had served with such loyal joy.
        Was felled because
Had frightened the milksop boy
        Of a doting jarl.
The dotings began to cloy
        When the gloating babe—
Did I ask him to watch so near?—
        Was crushed by my crash.
I was sawed to serve as his bier.

4.

        Years crawled by,
More slow than the worms in my fruit,
        Till coffin-ghouls
Smashed me to look for loot.
        Burghers came:

"This lid will stanch our boat."
        Not quite. The leak
I wrought proclaimed I frowned
        On lovers of trade.
The only man not drowned—

                5.

        —Was a thief in the brig
Who clung to my side while they sank.
        I wrought him dreams
Till he rose to a pirate-chief's rank.
        He knighted me
Death's epicure: Sir Plank.
        I wrought revolt;
He walked me, too. How sweet
        Are men's last squeals,
The fears I can taste through their feet.

                6.

        Gallows and crash,
Coffin and treacherous leak.
        Not bad in their way.
But these diving-board days are my peak.
        (*You must walk the plank.*)
Every man's tread is unique:
        Some grudging, some gay;
Some bouncing, some needing a shove.
        (*Here's goodbye, here's the edge of the edge of the plank.*)
I'll remember each footstep with love.

Cacti: *Paysage Moralisé*

Their health is parch. Their moral code is gash.
        Root-anchored only when you watch them,

They hop and clown behind you when you don't.
Older than sex, they grow by budding,
Oval on oval twigged of pulpier green.
A continuity of lobsters,
An ambuscade of velvet felinity:
Saharas crammed into a crouch.
Who will solve this charade of the cactus gauntlets,
This earned ouch of the heel of strut,
Who but hate's tenderness, the Eros of torture,
The mutuality of wounds?
Here grows a target where the barbs land facing
Outward,—a reverse Sebastian,
A retribution of boomerang porcupines.
Then teach, didactic vegetable,
How justly man is aimed at by his aims,
How in the archeries of ego
A target is a mirror is a scales.

2 : The Girl Menagerie

"Now kindness (wide-eyed as the dolls of girls),
Killed and redeeming, shines from all pale girls."

—page 21

To Womanly Beauty in Motion
(I. Ode.   II. Paean.   III. Threnode.)

I. Ode

1.

This way, that way, as distraction earns it,
Earthbound beauty, turning with her side-glance,
Jars the taffeta of statue-poise with
Harmonies of rumpling. Only odes are
Fool enough for praise that earns no swerving
Shoulder and dislodges not one pin.

Motion, motion ruffles brooks and sinews
Back from winter. Earthbound beauty pulses
Not in ageless ode but flick of side-glance.
Yawn at art, at soul, at bronze perfection;
Shiver at their mere eternity;
Warm us back into mortality,

Darling demagogy of the flesh.

2.

Bridge spanning seed and crop in one slow sweep,
Be sung; and never waste, to glance toward song,
The sensuous cataract your torso turns,—
Sinewing down from mobile pause of throat
To indolent cascades, then arch of marble
Quicksand, a bunched up gentleness of storm.

Outside, the harsher storm of nations threatens
Earthbound beauty. Sweetest when most bound,
Fallible human love in deluge-time:
I'll stay to drown with you if you will let me.

You'll waste no glance where, proffering their ice-floes
Of monumental deathlessness as rafts,

Ageless odes irrelevantly float.

ii. Paean

You were the May of them all, as concrete as delight.
Flowingness—shoulder and half-turn—of sun-slope all morning:
See how it, see how you—girl-turn—yes, see how your motion
Raveled, unraveled the rays of the slant of your hair.
Then everything slanted and sloped, and I mounted your stair,
And your rays melted wild into rivers; I played on that ocean.
Am implicated—since then—in each turn of your turning,
My garden an armful of noon through a winter of night.

iii. Threnode

1.

Bitter your cheek-lines, and I love you bitter.
No word stares more intense than rhymes with "bitter."
No glance more musical than bitterness.
Long-slanting winter-rays, half skidding, skitter
Across defeat. Their icy gold is bitter.
Through worlds where every grace must fray and fritter,
No badge more gallant than your bitterness.

2.

Neat, trim, and desperate in her travel-dress,
Love only half unpacked,—no queen on litter.
Accept love so: knitter, in turn, and splitter
Of two half-woven strands of bitterness.
To win is falser when to lose is fitter;
Love's flights are but an ineffectual flitter
Beside the wing-span earned by bitterness.

3.

The spy who broadcasts heart's iambic pitter-
Patter of code from underground transmitter,
Betrays our censored secret: bitterness.
Accept heart so, love even love's outwitter;
Hear, head on breast, the traitor-heart confess
That through the gamut lovers' bodies press,
Through all that shattering terror's tenderness,
The whiplash of their tensest truth is this:
Their winged and stinking ecstasy flows bitter.

4.

From flimsy twigs a sentimental twitter
Falls like false-notes across a courtier's kiss;
While these and those share summer's facile bless,
You share with me our holy bitterness.
Transfiguring with elegíac glitter
Sonorously a wintering caress,
Across that falling-note—that snow-word "bitter"—
Falls sunset's final, ceremonial tress.

(1964 version)

The Day's No Rounder Than Its Angles Are

(for Anya)

Mere dark is not so night-like as it seems.
The night's more silken than the dark by far.
So many dark things are not night at all:
The cupboard where the cakes and poisons are;
The coffin where old men get locked in dreams
Alive, and no one hears their knocks and screams;
Shadows; and lightlessness of curtain's fall.

The night is further than the dark is far.
The night is farness, farnesses that reel.
The day is nearness, nearnesses that jar.
The day's no rounder than its angles are.
But though its angles gash you with a wound
Invisible, each night is soft and round.

The night is softer than the dark is satin.
The night is softness, softnesses that heal
The many, many gashes where you bled.
The day is loudness, loudnesses that threaten;
An evil sexton-dwarf hides in your head.
Oh where escape his bells that peal and peal?

The night is stiller than the dark is dead.

1944

Hard Times Redeemed by Soft Discarded Values

1.

This was the summer when the tired girls
Breathed in the parks another planet's air
And stretched like hyphens between Here and There,
Stretched and lounged and yawned on every lawn.
Then did the planet of the tired girls
Whirl from the constellation named The Fawn
(Goodbye, mild star-light of the Sign of Fawn)
And ride into the galaxy named Fangs,
Where every dew-drop like a tear-drop hangs.
This was the summer-sob of wounded girls.

2.

This was the tiredness when summer's girls
Grew warm and hidden griefs like downy curls.

Then was the drowsy melody of Languish
(Goodbye, archaic waltzing-world of Languish)
Jazzed to the bad bad bad blues of Wild Anguish.
Serene old Mozart world—peace ethics laws—
Fades like girl-sighs. Or begs like kitten paws.
Or soars, unheeded like too faint a star,
Into the limbo where the tired are.
This was the faded June of fainting girls.

3.

Then came the gnats who feed on sad young girls,
Winging and stinging through the gauze of dusk,
Buzzing and burning all that summer night.
Then did all perfumes bitterly take flight
Out of the stylish cloying of Sweet Musk
(Goodbye, warm pensive world of sensuous musk)
Into the dark dark dream-flower named Take Fright.
Then girls discovered that their dolls were dead,
Hollow yet lovely like the gold skins shed
When locusts molt, found on old trees by girls.

4.

Now kindness (wide-eyed as the dolls of girls),
Killed and redeeming, shines from all pale girls.

Venice, 1945

Dies Illa *

*'Dies irae, dies illa
Solvet saeclum in favilla.'*

Everywhere
Awareness lurks behind a thousand blendings.
Awareness shivers—even in oases—

* Published by the *Harvard Advocate*, 1936, as winner of Harvard's 1934-35
Garrison contest for undergraduate verse.

At hard-riding portents saddled like thistledown
On winds that have strayed in many places,
Seen many forgotten beginnings and thrown
The dust of many great and little endings
  Into the air.

  Out of the air
Our swelling shadows breathe us when we breathe.
Sky snuffs up earth. Solidity has been rent.
A runaway outlaw nerve—or is it death?—
Signals and signals our brain-cells with
Black. In our sweetest entanglement,
When loam enriches or when limbs enwreathe,
  Who's purring there?

  Dead faces wear
An underwater strangeness, once so precious.
Our goggle-eyes plead upward—beached at birth—
To God. So minnows pray to beaks of gannets.
More air, more air!—the gasp of earth,
One of the uninhabitable planets,
Where meat stuffs meat (as food or love) yet threshes
  Alone when most a pair.

  But from God's stare
We're not alone, or is it death, unblinking?
My dear, we have strolled to a spell-bound place
Where sunflowers have eyes that follow us.
Twilight lisps at our knees to swallow us;
Don't move; we are watched by a cloud with a crafty face.
Move fast; the fingers of the sun are sinking
  And clutch your hair—

  And tug you beneath by your hair.
Sunset-defier, sharer of dawns, hold me so
Close I will never let you go,—
Clasping you free from all the ebb of things,
From all but One. And if the One outclings,

Let love not die alone; let springtime wilt:
All nature ambushed by one descending quilt
    Of sick air

    Everywhere thick.
And I—if it ends, if solidity ends tonight—
Will hold you close through all the holy thunder . . .
Till unrepentant flesh rekindles and, dawn-frenzied,
Strains at the quilt of sky and blazes through and rends it,
Shaking our windowpane with jubilant light.
You will shrug at God and with how young a wonder
    Wake me quick.

1932

Well Said, Old Mole

How frail our fists are when they bash or bless
The deadpan idiot emptiness of sky.
In this immortal hoax of time and space
(Our creeds and wisecracks equally awry)
We have no solace—no, nor soul—but by
The mortal gesture of a doomed caress:
Man's first and last and honorable reply.
Against the outer infinite, man weighs
The inwardness within one finite face
And finds all space less heavy than a sigh
And finds all time less lingering than *tendresse*.
We are alone and small, and heaven is high;
Quintillion worlds have burst and left no trace;
A murderous star aims straight at where we lie.
And we, all vulnerable and all distress,
Have no brief shield but love and loveliness.
Quick—let me touch your body as we die.

1945

In the Destructive Element Immerse

The hoodoo rodents of love's submarine
Are much too gray. Are publicly obscene.
No paws that burrow like love's submarine
Are furrier than certain waves have been;
But waves!—but like a gesture of abhorrence
Their corrugation rolls from love in torrents.

No minks that slither like love's submarine
Have pelts more glossy than the sea is sheen;
But sea!—it spews, it sheds these gray pollutions
By always beaching love, their carrier.
Spiraling down and up through brine and air,
Love's valves become involved in convolutions;
And all descent is gray.
                    But rich.
                    But rare.

1946

For Two Girls Setting Out in Life

'The two young ladies separated. Juliette, who wanted to become a grand lady, how could she consent to be accompanied by a girl whose virtuous and plebeian inclinations might dishonour her social prestige? And Justine, for her part, how could she expose her good name to the companionship of a perverse creature who was looking forward to a life of vile lewdness and public debauchery? They bade each other an eternal adieu, and next morning they both left the convent.'–Marquis de Sade, *Justine, or The Misfortunes of Virtue*, 1791.

I

The sick man, though, had wit who thought you up.
Who can not picture you that fatal morning?
Homeless, not even knowing where you'll sup,
You sigh, 'Adieu' and ask yourselves, 'What next?'
I sound like old Polonius–don't be vexed
If I give too avuncular a warning;
But having scanned your futures in a text,
I gasp at all the ways you'll be misled
(Your nuns behind you and your males ahead)
And want to save you from your author's plot.
When he says, 'Follow me,' you'd better not.

II

Justine, by all means do be virtuous
But not in so provocative a fashion.
I'm being frank; please listen: solely thus
Can you elude that lamentable passion
For which your author lends his name to us.
The night he ties you down in Bondy Wood,
You'll learn what happens to the gauchely good.

III

Yet you'll endure, Justine. Most stubbornly.
To love mankind, to preach tranquillity
To Etna or reverse a spinning planet
By bleating trustfully your Pauline tracts—
Such supernatural smugness is sheer granite:
No, not eroded by whole cataracts
Of fondlers groping through—beyond—your body
To sate in flesh the spirit's old distress
And plunge their seekings in some final sea.
Meanwhile, far off, a certain chic Grand Lady
Half-hears a voice each night (too kind for spleen)
That weeps for all her daytime wilfulness:
'Juliette! Juliette! What have you done to me?
It's I—your other self, your poor Justine.'

IV

And you, Juliette: have fun while doing ill.
Be un-immaculate *while yet you may*
(I drop this hint to give the plot away).
But when you dance with sweating stable-lads
Or tired Dukes who giggle at your skill,
Don't think it's you who dance; the ghosts of gods
Who died before our oldest gods were young,
Twirl savagely in your polite salon:—

That sofa where reclining comes so easy,
Is far more haunted than you'll ever guess.
Your lips raise shrines as mystic as Assisi
From whiteness they so piously caress.
O you are very wise (your playful nights,
That seem so casual, are primordial rites)
And very silly (promise me you'll stay
A pretty little girl who'll never spell
'Chthonic' nor learn her Freud too sadly well).
Last week I think I met you on Broadway.

V

Two truths, two sisters. An obsessive pair:
Serene in their unalterable roles
Whether their frantic author flog or kiss them.
And either truth rebukes our limbo where
Girls are not Bad but merely Indiscreet,
Girls are not Good but merely Very Sweet,
And men are filed in their own filing-system
With frayed manila-folders for their souls—
Once labelled GOD'S OWN IMAGE: USE WITH CARE
But now reclassified as OBSOLETE.

Justine! Juliette! We need you, both of you,
'Girls of mild silver or of furious gold.'
Revoke your spat; it is our own feud, too.
You smile? Yet you can bless us if you will.
And then, and then—identities unveiled,
Tall tales rehearsed and poutings reconciled—
      Two opposites will find each other
      And sob for half a day together;
For heaven and hell are childhood playmates still.

1947

The Aphrodite Trilogy

I. *The Ripple at Cythera*

Blue silence. Thickening. Then the long slow ripple.
The waves lobbed one shared language at the headlands.
Who'd guess a girl-child's relevance to harvests?
Yet the nudged beach quivered
A consternation of breast-pale dances.
And from the shoreline up the dunes, a rumor:

"With muffled fins a saboteur has landed.
But no, not fins; only a calcified Oh,
A nothing, a housed echo." Who'd guess pulse there?
The first boy who pocketed the first
Sea shell, knapsack of wounds,
Was smuggling inland the singing birthpangs,
Staining the dry hills with droned foam.
Calamitous sweetness,
What purer wisdoms once walked a loveless earth?
Does loam hoard reveries from feverless ages
Before that flabbergasting lilt was born?
No land-sound but was changed forever after,
Rubbing with a new reverberation
The sheens of bloom, the taffetas of wind,—
Riddling the rhythms of the works of man
With added resonance of
Undertow.

II. *Invocation*

Undertow,
You other blue,
Tow these to you.
Came sky; in upside-down of sky, there always
Was undertow.
Came Greek year; shrines held only what a port can
Of undertow.
Came eons, Lilith, Venusburg; there always
Was undertow.
Queened, demoned, pseudo-tamed, renamed, there always
Was undertow.
Lines of the straighteners (grid of nerves and subways)
Are coming; indestructible below
Is undertow.
Them, goddess, too,
Swerve not too late from where they hurtle to;
Sway up unearned—for these who earn the arson—
The olive too.

III. *Voice from Below*

You poked apart the sleepwalk poise of things.
Your own sleep now
     won't seal you from our waking.
God? No, but gods!—who'd strip for mere abstract ones?
Obscenely shrine, piously desecrate us,
Our swelling fruit half terror half decorum,
Flesh flushed with spilling wine: we touchable gods.
  . . . I still am I, the mussed-up goddess,
  Starlight and pond-scum tangled in a ditch.
  What I've arrived to bring, is not salvation—
  Too much of that too loud too many eons—
  But choice between two fires: love's and arson's;
  And each one pulsing, pulsing through all shields.
  Lively is not alive; a funeral pyre
  Is snugger than a hearth a little while.
Here comes a cypress jury-grove to judge
Your backtalk to the southwind. You have made,
By your definings and unsorceries,
The fig cloacal and the fountain chemic,
Whereby a sky's whole constellation crashed.
For this the Courts of Eros sentence you
To health,
   and to drum-majorettes,
      and to
Your nightly screaming when my pulse throbs through.

      —*From* The Tree Witch, *1961*

The Second Try

Goethe: "The eternal feminine draws us onward."

1.

Make me a world, girl; make as terra made;
Be she, be starting over what went stale.
One fingertip of femininity—
To pat what musses and to flounce what twirls—
Could spruce whole planets up. The god-spell then:
One minute long you have to groom a globe
Any old kind of way. Start fussing; wish.
Your slightest fidget reigns; I don't know why
Except that life's been loaned a second try.

2.

A coaxing of cupped palms—just so—from clay,
Dark sting of cheeks, strict wildness of the voice,
And now all's underway. Already swamp
Twists free—all palm and saurian—out of sea;
Your reeking, waddling firstlings play. Enough!
Now sponge the slate, make room for—use your fancy
What to make room for. Monsters cleared away,
Build phoenix, pegasus, and unicorn;
Hurry, don't waste brief godhood; build them, plan
Such symbols of your role as Muse to man.

3.

At once kaleidoscopes of matter rattle
A second chance the second time around.
Swamps groan, hills labor, new life comes to life
Beyond old dowdy domesticities.
But what familiar sound is this (cluckcluck)?

30

Incredible priestess, stop!—what have you loosed?
With housewife-fingers, buxom terra tidies
A landscape for gallina of the roost.

Girl-Child's House

I

Less like an eggshell than a tourniquet.
Outside it: all that made the wind so knowing.
Inside it (being just a house): just she.
Her pillow was a summer of old porches.

That door in those days meant so much to her
It frightened her the time its slamming breeze
Fluttered her blouse as if it *knew* of breasts.
Then she drew subtler pressures to her, softer

Bruises by lolling cool on flames of grass.
Kicking her shoes off, careless where they landed,
She spread her toes as wide apart as ducks do
To let the wind-webs through that never came.

When pairs of vermin-wildness serenaded
With wooden grunts, her porch stayed white and airy;
Stayed paceable as cake-like castle-walls
To which all hoofbeats soar that never come.

Until one day they came.

II

Two loitered round and round the wire netting
Of the verandah as the shadows lengthened.
November rising; wings and fountains setting.
She leaned an arm on his and raised it strengthened.

Is it because she found her park forlorner,
Green thinned to needles, yellow basking vaster,

That she strayed pale and puzzled, like a mourner?
She drifted slowly, slowly, breathing faster.

She raised her chin as if to wish sky's falling.
As if all sky were only one kiss more.
But, twisting, heard two ferrets caterwauling.
And wrenched into the house. And locked the door.

The Paintbrush of the Old Ones

When membrane of milady's sleep
Doth learn the courtesy of how to fray
As nobly as the pounded ice
Relinquishes its immemorial pool,
     Then come the gallopers of sleep.
     No plummet asks how deep they rule
     Who once rode ponies out of stone-age skies
     To hunt the mammoth for his wool.
On caves of her they paint their fuzzy prey.
On membrane of milady's sleep.

Playing

Playing in the dark for hours with the fisherman's wife,
Until the quicksand held him like a net,
     Carlos laughed with delight.
Then sensed a cold and daytime kind of net
     And laughed with fright:
     "More excitable her flesh
     Than mild-eyed fish
     Tonight, tonight
Whose guts this morning she cleaned out with a kitchen-knife."

3 : Earth

"Stay faithful to the earth, my brethren."
—From *Thus Spake Zarathustra*

"They imagine to perform bodily actions while in
fact they have no physical bodies but act in their
thoughts."

—Paracelsus

In the Month of March the Snails Climb Tender Trees

In the month of March the snails climb tender trees
To be nearer the Pleiades.
Grass fingers nab heat.
The fish jump for the fun of it.
Later the roses are willing to fall.
The wasted thistle-fluff isn't sorry at all.
A vineyard, met while walking, is a shelter
Good to hold to in that helter-skelter.
For fun—or food? or hooks?—life likes to twitch;
After the ice, it will not matter which.
After the ice, the feathers—once all throat—
Are shushed; the paraplegic lakes can not reach out.

And so, from hooked exuberance to numbed retreat,
The gamuts have no meaning; or what they have of it
Encysts in chunky particulars,—
The specific timothy-grass, the ungeneralized tears,
The vineyard met while walking, a life-buoy of Here,
Good to hold, in wave on wave of Anywhere.

Again, Again

Who here's afraid to gawk at lilacs?
Who won't stand up and praise the moon?
Who doubts that skies still ache for skylarks

And waves are lace upon the dune?
But flowering grave-dust, flowerlike snow-dust,
But tinkling dew, but fun of hay,
But soothing buzz and scent of sawdust
Have all been seen, been said—we say.

BANALITY, our saint, our silly:
The sun's your adverb, named "Again";
You wake us with it willy-nilly
And westward wait to tuck us in.
Trite flame, we try so hard to flout you,
But even to shock you is cliché.
O inescapable and dowdy.
O tedium of dawn each day.

Who's new enough, most now, most youngest
Enough to eye you most again?
Who'll love the rose that love wore longest,
Yet say it fresher than quick rain?
I'll see. I'll say. I'll find the word.
All earth must lilt then, willy-nilly,
Trapt by one golden banal chord
Of August, wine, and waterlily.

Stanzas in Love with Life and August

What can this wind do to these August leaves?
It folds their ears back on the shaggy bough.
Back, back and forward. Rippling weather-vane.
Does this, but nothing worse than this, although
Juggles them like a wave that jumps upon
Seven slower waves to pound apart their foam
In a thousand drops for still more later waves
To squeeze together in one undertow.

Apart, together; apart, together again;
Not once in August shall one leaf blow down.
Let winds be fiddled by the grass they comb;—
What else can winds do to these August leaves?
Green ankles, kick as crazy as you choose,
For none shall tumble until August does.

II

A pair of slight tennis shoes is hurrying by in August.

III

Here's life-besotted, writhing rhododendron,
Stretching its sinewy sap in every pore,
Drowsy and fierce, like a great carnivore
Lunging in one green leap upon the sun.
Untamed? Yet all its jungle-grossness fawns
Before two passing slight white cotton socks,
Disheveled perfume, and a burr-starred smock.
For an hour, peace and rage and the music of growth are one.

IV

Is hurrying by in August.

V

Inexhaustible waterfalls of green splash up
Crazily, in dark directions lavished,
Rippling through blue veins under cotton blouses
A resonance from flutes beneath the loam.
Down, death; down, dog;
Stop, wind; down, she said.
For one whole hour nobody can harm a leaf.

VI

Hurrying by in August.

VII

The winds? Can only harm what's pale and outward;—
How dark and deep the green of August glows!
What can a wind do to an August leaf?

For an hour, kick just as crazy as you choose.
"But if you hear far unseen apples thud?"
What is it to us? Those cannot tug us down,
This being August.

August, glow slow, glow long.

VIII

Hurrying by.

IX

(Vulnerable August, deaf to all but fountains.)
She paused. Who hoped and touched? She hurries by.
She wears a blouse of cotton summerwhite
—(Is it fountains, listen, or the first torn fruit?)—
And tennis shoes.

X

Can you see a thud, can you hear green fading?
Glow slowly, holy foliage; apple-red is
Unasked for in this flute-fed, loam-thick hour.
. . . Another thud; closer.
Menace is the name of the small breeze between the leaves.
. . . Closer.

XI

Turning-point.
A pair of slight tennis shoes hurries by in August.

XII

How dark, how deep the green of August glows!
Thinks not of all the death it fed upon.
Thinks not of all the life its death will feed.
One hour—O deepening foliage, sweep of lawn,
Heavy green of August—pause before you're gone.
Life-scented, knee-deep-hugging, eerie grass,
Good bluegreen spruce, free unpruned hedge and heath,
Calm moss, wait long. Glow long enough for us,

Petal of the pond-scum, drowner's floating wreath,
Whose bees are frogs in emerald flowers. Slow moss,
Glow long. Deep-breathing, flush-cheeked August, bleed
Your ebb's arterial green in slower tide
Back down into the loam you lean upon.
We pause as long an hour as August does;
Crisscrossed in dark directions overhead,
Hot comets hurt each other as they pass;
Cold moles grub past each other underneath;
All pause as short an hour as August does.
Eyes have met eyes while all that green stood still;
Though it took but one small breeze to burst that spell,—
When eyes pass eyes as dark as August glows,
Eyes shall glance backward after August goes.

Nostalgia

(for a while it was good to have been the word "man")

1.

After eight thousand years among the stars,
    A sudden wistfulness for August
    Tugged me—like guilt—through half a cosmos
    Back to a planet sweet as canebrake,
    Where winds have plumes and plumes have throats,
        Where pictures
Like "blue" and "south" can break your heart with sweet suggestiveness.

2.

After a mere eight flickers, nothing changed there
    Among the birds, still just as blazing,
    Among the rain of leaves on rivers,
    The heartbreak of the south and blue,

The canebrake-sweet of August night;
But only
The people changed, my people, oh my people, my forgetters.

3.

"After eight cycles, how is this you greet me?
Where is my horse? Where is my harp?
Why are the drums of goat-skin silent?
Spin my abyss of resin-wine;
Drape me my cloak of prophecy;
My name is . . ."
And then I said the true and lost and terrifying word.

River

1.

Around the curve where all of me that fountained
Leans over on its side and is a stream
And loiters back the long, the round-about,
The sweet, the earth way back to sea again—
At just that curve I woke.
                    What is awakeness?
A thing I own? Or opened eyes that own me,
Sobbing me through as if my banks were lids?
I only know I'm freed to be less free:
A tear of longing on a cheek of loam.

2.

Before that flash, I sleepwalked through my cycle
(Sea, fountain, stream, then waterfall to sea)
While never feeling how it feels to feel.
I have no memory of what came before

40

Except a sandy silver sense of glide.
Who took flow's casualness? I never asked
To symbolize or mean. Who took my sleep?
Leaves fall on me as light as sunbeams; even
Boulders are weightless; only meanings weigh.
I am a river and a river only.
But now, since waking, not of water only.
A tic of knowing on a cheek of time.

3.

A surface-skimming stone of half-intrusion
Taints with one older wince my younger rapids,
One changeless wound of things: that all things change.
That ripple rumples the affirming pages
Of solid hills
        and wriggles (like a stain)
A question-mark across their paper truth.

4.

Sea, fountaining the earth way back to sea.
Sea-cloud to rainfall, waterfall to sea.
I am the sling-shot. No, I am the sling.

5.

Faster. I skid between the rocks like wind
Between the leaves. I skim the rocks so lightly
I now seem less a river than a breath.
Or is this hurtling airiness a signal
(How can I know yet, being so young awake?)
That I have reached my final waterfall?
Too late to stop; slave-bound by back and forth,
My cycle bounces between sea and sky.
No rest for me in either blue; my tiptoes
Of dew creep up and stub against the clouds;
And clatter down again; again to climb.
Green-drifting pools and lulls below, goodbye;
Intimate river-bed, joy of the touch of a contour,

Clinging to me you never will climb with me now.
Stay with me seaward: earth-half of my cycle.
But skyward (stript of shores, a ghost of vapors)
Each moves alone. And now I flex my sinews
For stream's last jump—I clear the rocks—I fall
To rise.

6.

No, not yet fall, not rise, but hover
A motionless instant. Wrenched beyond all patterns,
Suspended free, I am the world's first morning
(Everything possible, uncommitted sinews)
And stream's first jump.
                        The hover ends. I move.

1965

Fiftieth Birthday

Only less sure of all I never knew.
Always more awed by what is never new.
Computer, spare the mustang's randomness.

There was an oracle. On Samothrace?
There have been tablets. Here? Some greener place?
I (leaf) paint leaves that (falling) try to dance.

Have seen the big death, felt the little death:
The icy and the April breathlessness.
And understand them less and less and less.

Have met the loam-fed and the plastic wreath:
Statesman and hack. Two frightening frightened boys.
Both more endearing than the consequence.

Have heard your rebels and have heard your guild:

And still can't tell the standard from the stance
When both are so rehearsed a cheering noise.

Have squandered silver and have hoarded pence.
Have watched the ant-hill build, burn up, rebuild
(The running is and isn't meaningless)

At Ilium. Or will it be South Bend?
I'll grudge the run a meaning in the end
When wounds that might wound back or else "transcend"

Have risked—instead—to be. Not even bless.

                                                          1966

The Outward Life

(freely transplanted from Hofmannsthal's *Ballade des Aeusseren Lebens*)

And children still grow up with longing eyes,
That know of nothing, still grow tall and perish,
And no new traveler treads a better way;

And fruits grow ripe and delicate to cherish
And still shall fall like dead birds from the skies,
And where they fell grow rotten in a day.

And still we feel cool winds on limbs still glowing,
That shudder westward; and we turn to say
Words, and we hear words; and cool winds are blowing

Our wilted hands through autumns of unclutching.
What use is all our tampering and touching?
Why laughter, that must soon turn pale and cry?

Who quarantined our lives in separate homes?
Our souls are trapped in lofts without a skylight;
We argue with a padlock till we die,

In games we never meant to play for keeps.
And yet how much we say in saying: "twilight,"
A word from which man's grief and wisdom seeps

Like heavy honey out of swollen combs.

1947

Gray Hair

An old man with flowers
Is lament without sorrow;
Delighted dust
Perpetrates noon.
Sound of reaping
Even in springtime
Sings inside me
Without sorrow.
Soft wind,
I am not afraid to die.

The Reaching Out of Warmth Is Never Done

The reaching out of warmth is never done.
To see around the bend, to see around,
Through ice to see a poppy wink you on,
Entangle with the tentacles of light
And nudge a green unkemptness up from night,—
The mixed-up splice of things, the all, the one.
        Mix in, mix in, and weave a blurring Other.

Give all—keep twining in—and you may get
A more-than-all: three dance a strict quartet,
And pairs are threes (O Eros, unseen brother),
And even grapes, so single in their glowing,
Mix with a twin from sky (O wine-god, flowing);
The reaching out of warmth is never done.
What reaching up, though old, can still astound?
Persephone is stirring underground.
Stretching up drowsily through melting snow,
See how each calyx opens, row on row
(Whole hillsides now, soon half a planet sighing);
Each flower-throat "O" exhales her wakening yawn.
What twining in with death is never dying?
Till flame is burnt and water drowned,
The reaching out of warmth is never done,—
The mixed-up blur of gods, the good black sun.

In Earth Who Wallows Like Its Borrowers?

My tryst with romany: black eyes and white
Teeth of the palest, blackest-haired of daughters.
Henna you prinked by Andalusian waters,
Dawdling—with scorn's grace—south of wrong and right.
        O you
Laughed sun back hundredfold like caressed dew.

And did you, past my sonant fruit-tree strolling,
Hear hundred wines of air compel you back?
Then what a mist of longing our enfolding!—
Fused hoax of dew and wine, each other's lack.
        O may
Coastlines of contour rise from mistiest spray.

No cosmic wrangles crowning either Prince,
Not all the stakes of soul for which They clash,
Are worth the angel of a lucky glance
That casual earthlings in their glittering flesh
      O throw
At daily things,—rain's tilt, or sheen of snow.

In earth who wallows like its borrowers?
What bodies can so sensuously press
As masks of unborn shadows? Fallowness
Can yearn the very sun loose from its course.
      O would
That ghosts, through love, earned shape. If but we could.

I know you now! No romany your home.
Then know me too; no arcady my lair.
Formless you flash; I hope you, and you are.
Weightless I hover; need me, and I loom.
      O we
Never were. Homeward to hell come flee.

4: Sky

"For what is a song for
If not to stretch hands out
To signal the falling,
'You're never alone'?"

—*page 63*

Last Day of Childhood

You cannot bear this silent, heavenly sadness.
You need voluptuous, need tellurian sighs.
Not up but down, down, earthward is your sky,
Your own (but how to make you know?) by birth.
There shines the park that offers you more lilacs
Than all the arms of longing can enfold.
And so you grow, you grope for parks while drifting
All the while southward all unknowingly.
Then groves more south, more slow than lukewarm breezes
(More south, more velvet) sing you dissonances
(More dense, more south) that cloy unbearably,
Till every vibrant, swaying twig bends down
Heavy with figs and with the grapes of breasts.

2.

Such exhalation, then, of tenderness—
Of fondling tides on crumbling promontories,
Of shade of clouds on white young birch-bark, fleeting
As patterns hinted on the wildest grasses
By rims of bicycles in picnic weather—
Slakes you to sleepiness. You snuff the sun out;
You unroll far beaches to your chin like quilts.
You become a *Maerchen* dreamed by the deep, cool clams,
And by the huddling bats of timeless caves.
Eight hundred years of this. And then a signal.
You'll know, you'll never doubt it, you'll arise;
And, yawning, stretch into a constellation;
And fill the sky that has been waiting for you.

Gladness Ode

Because you made me glad, I was the net.
"Why do you haunt me?" asked the midnight lake.
    "To fish," I said, "that rounded fire.
        Am not afraid to fall."

No, though that halo moved and moved and moved,
It could not hide from me for all its slyness.
    (Beneath the waters warningly
        Moon's Icaruses sprawl.)

High watchers glowed their pity on the lake:
"To wear mere mirrored circle like a crown,
    Is it for this the young men drown?"
        But I, being net, must haul.

Before you made me glad, I feared such splashing;
Futile invoker then: "Dive me-ward, moon."
    But now it's I who dive defiant
        Cold curves like a ball.

The lake sang out a grace-note scrawled by stars.
I was the net, and all my strands were glad.
    I pulled the moon out of the water.
        It wasn't heavy at all.

To My Isis

Death never was my king; I stalled his powers
Ten years by dollars and by doctors. Even

That time when he outflanked me, iced and shriven,
A traffic jam held up my hearse for hours.

And anyway, *who cares* how much he shuffled
My ripped off wrappers—fanning forth from man
To worm and back, through his accordion-span—
So long as soul, perched safe, smirks down unruffled?

Don't *you* smirk likewise; true, I'm all awry,
I'm dust, I stick to every whim like lint;
I'm dandelion fluff; my gold spikes dry
And silver off with every aimless wind.

True, I'll admit I'm hard to recognize.
Agreed, that lunglessness clogs up the gears
Of diction. When I sing into your ears,
It seems your own lone loneliness that sighs.

It seems, it seems. Yet isn't. Must one pinch you
(Could I but slough a hand back) to convince you?
Could I laugh back a leg or two, you'd guess
I wear what most kicks out with liveliness.

I wear whatever shimmers . . . birch or trout.
My motes traipse far; I gawk from every spark—
And glow through mill-towns, intersect with soot,
And weave a flabbergasting sunny dark.

Enough of spirit! Mud I also mimic:
Let salivating wart-hogs gambol by,
Preening their bristles. All gross masks I'll try
But hairy spiders. These I still can't stomach.

Then, by grotesqueness purified, I strew
My soul in all that's delicate and pendant:
In petals and in ear-rings, sighs and dew—
Four trailing manes of comet-thoughts, ascendant

Toward airiness. . . . Up there, I'm sky-plants named
"Flowering Nostalgia," rooted firm in clouds;

My leaves droop with compassion; on each maimed
Comet they drop (like an embrace) kind shrouds.

How changed! And yet, where love is, how the same!
Just like Osiris—such a fancy name;
If it's no chore to patch him, it's no shame
To do as much for me; you should feel flattered.

I'm just as real as you are . . . merely scattered.

Looking Up Again and Again While Walking

(for Gertrude Norman)

1.

Was ever blue such undespairing blue?
Familiar sweep of perfect careless brows:
What else but she, translated into sky?
One summer I had a sister used to tilt
Her head a little in a haze of ease,
Without a wish, like that blue sleep up there.

2.

Was ever sky such haste-dissolving sky?
Just be (she hinted), be; don't wake, don't wish.
Her peace, too light a gift to seem redemption—
Like dewfall, uninsistent—shimmered twice:
From brows of flesh at first and then of air,
To her own self enough; yet more, yet more.

3.

My sister moved where words stopped short, recording
But this: there stones in any ditch have wings,
There weight combs back like clouds, there will lets go.

I used to try to sing her to my clay;
She used to try to pray me to her sky;
Then dawns and wishes bustled loud between.

4.

And now no longer? Passage through? This morning
My vision shakes like awe that has no object,
Feeling a new and nameless cycle near.
No blaze—God, God I beg—no blaze for one
Soul-sick too often of too garish sun.
. . . No blaze, no dawn descends, but fever's end.

Lot's Wife

Only her gape (that wistfulness) still lingers:
Whiteness unsweltered by an eon's suns.
Still backwards juts the gesture's frozen bronze,
Carved by Jehovah's cataclysmal fingers.

The tiny stinging snows that tears are made of—
Intolerable compression welds them here.
How shall she cry who is herself a tear?
Her retinas hold all she is afraid of:

The towns He hates, the scene that petrifies.
These sockets cannot spill four thousand years
Of visible terror. One taut muscle veers
Just at her throat-line. All that fire is ice.

Homewards. The hopeless turn; the shy regret;
Earth's faces jammed against His windowpane.
Not glass—it's faces shatter always then.
The spindrift awe of Hart's obsessive pet

Seal; or Aeneas on the boat from Troy

53

Before harps cooled the arson into art;
Not Elba's but Saint Helen's Bonaparte;
Each backwards
                    inward
                              like the salt-girl's eye.

The Modern Litany

(this positive-edited digest of Great Books is to be chanted with solemn
pause at end of each line)

Polls, charm schools, toilet trainers, lend us your deafness
To prejudice and make us nonconformists
Like everybody else. Tell Sparta
These truths we hold to be semantic blurs.
For we are alone among mankind
In combining free individualism (that is, personalized stationery)
With sense of community (our folk-dance classes).
Lead us not into deviation, but
Make us feel guilty near No Trespass signs
As we make guilt-ridden those who trespass against us.
Give us this day our daily treadmill
Of keeping up with those who keep more up.
But deliver us from psychosomatic heart-attacks
By granting free parking to customers. For thine is
The working-hypothesis that moves the sun and the other stars.

Ode to Joy

An die Freude
Seid umschlungen, Millionen!
Diesen Kuss der ganzen Welt!
Brüder—überm Sternenzelt
Muss ein lieber Vater wohnen.
              —voice of 19th-century humanism

1.

At the edge of the city,
Where birch and oak burst asphalt,
No longer son of gods,
    Not yet godless,
    The man of the city
Stands between acre and asphalt,
Hears in his pulse the far ones,
    Near as in sea-shells.

2.

He is a grandson.
"Better fully a robot"
(He is a grandson lamenting)
    "Than half-way a sky-born.
    I, child of
The clang-bang progress-promise,
I am more *from* than *to*.
    Help me, music."

3.

The softer trees
Are good for making music,
"Not son but grandson of tides,

55

Half flesh, half metal
At the edge of the city:
Remember we loved you; remember
To hear our tide inside you.
    Claim your birthright."

4.

        At the edge of exhaustion
The man holds on to sky.
The man holds on alone,
        Far from the near ones.
        The harder trees
Are good for making axes. . . .
"I can hold on no more.
        Grandfathers, kill me."

1964

Mary, Mary

(a four-volume Ph.D. thesis on Rousseau and original sin)

Mary, long by Boss's kisses bored,
Quit desk and stole His yacht and jumped aboard.
Her lamb took she, for purer were his kisses.
Compass and pistol took she in her purse.
Free sailed she north to eat new freedom up.
And her helped ocean and grew calm and snored.
But when with bleating chum she cuddled up,
Unleashed His typhoons Boss; therein no bliss is.
Then knew she—by four signs—whose jig was up:—

Her buoyed the life-preserver down, not up;
True was the pistol's aim, but in reverse;
The compass steered, but only toward abysses;
The little lamb nipped Mary's thighs and roared.

The Three Impacts of Auschwitz

I. Crass Times Redeemed by Dignity of Souls
II. From Ancient Fangs
III. To Be Sung

. . .

I. Crass Times Redeemed by Dignity of Souls

1.

The music of the dignity of souls
Molds every note I hum and hope to write.
I long to tell the Prince of aureoles—
Groper-in-clay and breather-into-dolls,
Kindler of suns, and chord that spans our poles—
What avalanche of awe His dawn unrolls.
Then lips whose only sacrament is speech,
Sing Him the way the old unbaptized night
Dreads and
        needs and
                lacks and
                        loves the light.
May yet when, feigning poise, I overreach,
When that high ripening slowness I impeach,
Awe of that music jolt me home contrite!

O harshness of the dignity of souls.

2.

The tenderness of dignity of souls
Sweetens our cheated gusto and consoles.
It shades love's lidless eyes like parasols
And tames the earthquake licking at our soles.
Re-tunes the tensions of the flesh we wear.

57

Forgives the dissonance our triumphs blare.
And maps the burrows of heart's buried lair
Where furtive furry Wishes hide like moles.
O hear the kind voice, hear it everywhere
(It sings, it sings, it conjures and cajoles)
Prompting us shyly in our half-learnt rôles.
It sprouts the great chromatic vine that lolls
In small black petals on our music scrolls
(It flares, it flowers—it quickens yet controls).
It teaches dance-steps to this uncouth bear
Of skywardness who wears our skins as stoles.

The weight that tortures diamonds out of coals
Is lighter than the frisking hooves of foals
Compared to one old heaviness our souls
Hoist daily, each alone, and cannot share:
To-be-awake, to sense, to-be-aware.
Then even the dusty dreams that clog our skulls,
The rant and thunder of the storm we are,
The sunny silences our prophets hear,
The rainbow of the oil upon the shoals,
The crimes and Christmases of creature-lives,
And all pride's barefoot tarantelle on knives
Are but man's search for dignity of souls.

3.

The searcher for the market price of souls,
Seth the Accuser with the donkey head,*
Negation's oldest god, still duns the dead
For these same feathery Egyptian tolls—
But now, bland haggler, deprecates his quest
(The devil proving devils can't exist).
His boutonnière is a chic asphodel;
He makes Id's whirlpool seem a wishing-well,
Reflecting crowns to outstretched beggar-bowls.

* The donkey god Seth or Set, on the tombs of Egypt, seems to have been
history's earliest recorded name for evil; souls were his fodder.

58

No horns; no claws; that cheap exotic phase
Belonged to his first, gauche, bohemian days.
The nice, the wholesome, and the commonplace
Are Trilbys he manipulates in jest
Till their dear wheedlings subtly swerve our goals:—

MASK ONE: an honest, cleancut, sporting face
Such as will cheer for wrong with righteous grace,
Hiking in shorts through tyranny's Tyrols.

MASK TWO: a round and basking babyface
Distracts our souls, so archly does it beg,
Upblinking like a peevish pink poached-egg.

THIRD MASK: his hide-out is an aging face
That waits for youth in mirrors like an ambush
And lives our ardent "when"s as yawning "if"s
And, puffing corncobs, drawls between two whiffs,
"Why stick your neck out? Nonsense never pays,"
And rends our aspirations like a thornbush.
Unmasked on tombs by shrieking hieroglyphs,
Seth was his true—his hungry—donkey face,
Nibbling our souls as if their groans were grass,
This grazer on the dignity of souls.

4.

He, the huge bridegroom of all servile souls,
Swaps little jokes with little envious trolls
To snuff the radiance of tragedy
And vend us pleasure, which turns out to be
An optimistic mechanized despair.
O hear the glib voice, hear it everywhere
(It shouts, it shouts, it cadges and cajoles).
It feeds the earthquake fawning at our soles.
It hands out free omnipotence as doles.
Replaces tall towns with still deeper holes.
To make us God, needs just one hair's-breadth more.

The Agents said, "All ungregarious souls

Are priggish outlaws, stubborn Seminoles."
With confidential chats and heart-felt skoals,
As grinning as the reefs around atolls,
They nudged us each:
                    "You are alone, you are
The last, you are the lost—come flee—you are
The straggling warrior of the lost last war
To vindicate the dignity of souls."

5.

We answered: "Tell the Prince who brays at souls,
Your long-eared Lord who has strange crowns to sell,
That all his halos have a sulphur smell;
And though they flash like flying orioles
Or lure like bonfires on mountain knolls,
These gaudy girandoles are
                              blackness still."

Torn out of blackness, soon to choke on black,
Leaning on nothingness before and back,
Tight-lashed to lies by veins and nerves and Will,
My life is darkness. Yet I live to tell
What airy skeleton of shimmer strolls
From flesh that guards its consciousness of souls.
Then love, that gives and gives and loves the more,
Frees us the way the good and daily light
Heals and
          shreds and
                      liberates the night.
Though blinking—burning—shivering in the white
Blaze that each dust-heap blest with speech extols,
May every dark and kindled "I" revere
In every "you" that selfsame fire-core,
In every soul the soul of all our souls.

1944–46

II. From Ancient Fangs

(The time of this poem is in the far future, shortly after peace and love return to earth.)

1.

Like lamp of intricate stained glass which hangs
      From curved blue ceiling,
A fat bright-bellied insect hangs up there.
      At night, on traveler,
It drops like rich and heavy poison welling
      From ancient fangs.

2.

That insect's not the only thing which falls.
So many things must fall in their short day.
Careers and wine-cups; bombs and tennis-balls.
Even the sun. But sky? The sky must stay.

But now the sky itself is caving in.
O good old sky, O lid that keeps us snug,
Dear blue in which we always used to trust
As in the nurse our childhood bullied so,
When comfort was to see her loyal grin,
Ugly and safe, beam down on us below:
Dear sky, we pray to you, hold on, you must!
Hold tighter, sky. Be roof to us, not rug.

3.

"It seems I'm being prayed to: I
      Am sky,
Older than hours and than miles more far,
      Your spectator.
When worlds grow honest, noble, clean, or clever,
      I fall and smother them forever.
To keep your blue roof high, stop being good.
      All sights bore Me now but blood.

The main thing is to kill. And kill. And kill.
          First with your bullets. Then with steel.

"And when steel breaks, with hands and stumps of hands.
And when you've killed all strangers, kill your friends.
And if you've used up humans, stone a rat.
Call it a whim—I like My world like that.
It's your world, too. The only world you'll get."

4.

"At school they never used to talk like You."
          "No, not like Me."
"People back home don't want such things to do."
          "Perhaps. We'll see."
"Men won't splash harmless blood just for Your thirst."
          "No, not at first."

1946

III. To Be Sung

1.

If blossoms could blossom
One petal of petals
To whom all other blooms are
As leaves are to flowers,
It would be to the others
As you are, my daughter,
To all other daughters
Whom songs are adoring.
For what am I here for
If not to make love-songs
Of all the world's beauty
Whose birthday we share?

2.

If purest of fragrances
Brewed a quintessence
Too delicate-lonely

62

To ever be breathed,
It would be to the others
As you are, my daughter,
To all other daughters
Whom songs are encircling.
For what am I here for
If not to weave lassoes
Of song for the lonely
To tug them to love?

3.

Say yes to the breezes.
If any dishevels
One curl of a ringlet,
I'll know and be with you.
The grace-notes that feather
The wing-beats of longing
Are lead till they heal with
Their singing your crying.
For what is a song for
If not to smooth ringlets
Of daughters too hurt by
The prose of the world?

4.

When storms replace breezes,
No hurt can have healing.
Then the love I now sing you
Can pillow your fading.
For what am I here for
If not to link fingers
With daughters whose wistfulness
Worlds never answer?
For what is a song for
If not to stretch hands out
To signal the falling,
"You're never alone"?

5.

When the Camp says: "Dig graves now,
We're coming to shoot you,"
I'll help with your shovel
—(I'll know and be with you)—
To give you more seconds
To look up from digging
To look at the sun while
I pillow the sand out.
For what is love here for
If not to smooth ditches
For all the world's daughters
Whose dying we share?

1950

5: Wars

"I hate, I despise your feasts, and I take no delight
in your solemn assemblies."

—Amos 5:21

Snow Against Rain

I. Urgencies

I bring a message from the rain.
The addressee is green.
My sister is estranged terrain.
The sister of my sister is my bride.

What hilled as waves, careens as hill.
Sun's bitterer name is snow.
I bring a message to a queen.
The leaves perk up and listen; I can go.

Too late to argue with the tide.
Too soon to warn the green.
My sister's sister's sun is snow.
Let me go.

1966

II. Trust

That toad I crushed to pack a hill
(To footstool for a queen
A throne beyond the tick of snow)
Is nothing. Blame the tide.

Accuse, accuse. But whom? Terrain
Spins neutral: white or green.
Sun bled to dusk behind a hill
A thousand clocks ago.

I didn't crush you, and you know it.
I did, but let me go.
I am nothing but the voice of rain,
No seesaw weight of tide.

(Snows are paw-print and no,
Rivers too knotted to run,
Petals too frozen to reign,
Open to none.

Rains are tulip and know,
Resins too sharp to rein,
All, all untied,
Opening to noon.

Girders of steel or of grain,
Rages of green,
Sink under hill, under heel:
Twigs of a nest of a wren.

Hill under hill under hill,
Rust over grain over steel,
Dust listening for rain:
All is tide.)

Warm rains, outsinging tide,
Earn back estranged terrain.
Frail pact. One wrenching note
And trust lets go.

The toad I crushed to pack a hill
To throne a sunless bride
To wait beyond the crush of snow
Has wrenched the voice of rain.

1967

Line Against Circle

I. Tempest or Music
II. The Two Again

. . .

I. Tempest or Music

1. (*a progress rhythm*)

Solidity rushes on.
You move in a moving maze.
Vertigo—praise it—alone
Stays. Cling to it tight.
Man is a flare-up of clay;
Shall he wait to be snuffed, shall he run?
"Run!" the windows invite;
"Express, expand while you may."
Man is a skidding of light
Bogging in clouds, a daze
Of longings and fruits, a stone
Thrown by thrower unknown.
Praise elation of flight.

2. (*a Tory rhythm*)

Solidity rushes on—
Brittle ghost at play—
Onto the window bars.
"Stand, wait!" they invite;
"Compress to the core while you may."
Center and farthest sun,
Thower and throw are one;

Pattern stays.
Alternate heart-beat of light
Grooms and dishevels stars.
Rest in that heart. Praise
Repose of flight.

Coney Island, New York, 1954

II. The Two Again

Came one, circling in islands.
Came one, striding from shores.
One spell is of silence.
One spell is of words.

Came one, condenser of intensities,
The be, the grow, the deafmute round of trees.
Came one committing lengthwise in his striding,
No ring of hiding, no abiding wall.

The first is perfect peace. But small, but small.
The second dives and falters,
Darer of waters and
Discoverer of everything but peace.

Came one inward in islands.
Came one outreached a wall.
Circle and line, the two and never twin.
Comes one, some day, doing and

Laughing at doing? Free from din
Of silence as of words?
When comes one perfect in islands
And loud and long on shores?

Aswan, Egypt, 1966

The Lost Self

Underground-rivers ripple.
Ripples are sometimes heard.
        "Child, don't hear them.
        Sit down, tea is served."

People get used to each other.
Sometimes this leads to harm.
        "Elsewhere. Here's a
        Potful; cover it warm."

Younger, were years more under?
Later, less haunted by blue?
        "Patience; soon now
        You will be deaf to them too."

Once in a lifetime, buried
Rivers fountain and call.
        "Child, child, hear the
        Daily kettle boil."

Once; and who follows, touches
Sand? Or gods? Or—tell!
        "Child, stop trembling;
        Porcelain cups may spill."

Children whom tides have altered
Live fierce and far. And drown?
        "Quick, move nearer.
        Tea is served, sit down."

Progress: Question and Answer

What do you see in the holy dread of the moonlight?
(Is it fire-lures dawdling on treacherous bogs?
Or a goat-leap you cannot quite glimpse through the fogs?
Or some slut of a goddess with red-eyed dogs
Hunting her lover, the moon?)
        "Clambakes, clambakes on cranberry bogs;
        Cans piled up to the moon."

What do you hear in the holy dread of the moonlight?
(Some stalker whose reverent pouncing Yes
Affirms new unicorns of delicate loveliness?
When he kills, is it true that his beautiful claws caress
A painting, a poem, a moon?)
        "Clambakes, clambakes on cranberry bogs;
        Hamburgers dimming the moon."

What do you feel in the holy dread of the moonlight?
(Are you drunk—till the hush of it chills your hair—
With the wager of man and his gay-tragic dare
To be moon of his own inner tide down here?
O pronounce me the wine of the moon!)
        "It's clambakes, clambakes on cranberry bogs;
        Gumdrops all over the moon."

Big Doings

1. (*voice of will and technics*)

Big doings! Engines
Still higher. Up there

Stars (golden and flying)
Challenge. Again, again
Up reaches will, male, steel.
      Paper-flimsy below
      Is grove-child's aimless aim:
      Trifle of squandered graces,
      Confetti of false starts,
      Ashcan of reveries.
O Bentham, builder of cities,
Has Eros bridged space, has
Play honed precision tools?
Unlaunchable was trance. Then
Launch engines. Doings!

2. (*voice of trance and play*)

One day men will get up before the sunrise,
Night-air still eerie with Aldébaran,
And gravely wear the pointed cardboard hats
(Spangled with cookie-shapes from astro-textbooks)
That dwarfs and jugglers caper in at fairs
To make the yokels gape at lore of stars.
And each hat pointing toward Aldébaran.
I say there are strong winds between the atoms,
Strong lonelinesses all around each textbook,
And these, that day, will blow your hats toward ashcans,
Will waft or dip them as the atoms frisk,
Pleading, "Aim nearer, nearer, tenderer;
Find more in less, the highest in the inmost."
      You'll rally back, O fatuous Man Invictus;
      How masterful you'll snag the winds of space
      Right through their manes and braid them into networks
      And engineer far lonesomeness away
      And knead cowed space into your cookie-dough.
      Then how they'll soar, the pointing hats will soar,
      Your hero-hats will stab Aldébaran.
      Then burn your corpses or the pigs will eat them,
      Because the graves that day shrug tombstones off
      And gape astounded at Aldébaran.

But I (because the much is in the little
And cosmos hangs upon a feather's fate)
Will twist my hat into a paper airplane
And aim it nearer than Aldébaran
And skim it round a yellow butterfly.

Athos or Assisi

I. Mount Athos
II. Incantation from Assisi

I. Mount Athos

The archimandrites in their mountain niches
    Are calling one another;
Like bells in separate steeples, each outstretches
    His bronze tongue to his brother.

On Macedonian hills these abbots kneel
    And rock till hilltops sway.
A goat-herd shudders as his pastures reel:
    "The archimandrites pray!"

Their beds are coffins, and their shirts are shrouds;
    They gash their palms with spears,
While virgin angels simper from the clouds,
    "Our lovers are so fierce."

Each archimandrite squats on his own peak
    And bellows at the skies.
Their beards are black and oily, long and sleek,
    And blow toward paradise.

These burly priests (for patience far too proud)
    Roar out at death's delay;

74

Their hairy claws are flexed and gouge at God
  To speed his judgment day.

Above Mount Athos, cranes (a migrant swarm
  From Egypt to the Alps)
Are snatched in flight; their blood is guzzled warm
  In wild convulsive gulps;

And then (beyond endurance drunk with lust)
  The archimandrites spill
Their sainthood out: through wombs of clouds they thrust
  Their tautness, tall with Will,

Straight up to heaven—where their earth-love spews.
  Then fluttering angel squads,
Calmed again, fold their wings, but now their eyes
  Fall when they meet God's.

II. Incantation from Assisi

1.

Yesterday, a rose.
Tomorrow, only a leaf the color of roses.
When a new sacrament is invented, eighth, an eighth,
Its name will be regret-that-undoes, an agent, marvelous, a magic:
To salvage foundered sincerities from reefs of desolate embracing,
To get, to get back
          by praising, by praising.

2.

Prayer, delicate,
          the vesper instant:
Fold, fold your hands till the air they prison
Changes to a dove as the great gongs shudder.
Clench it lightly and lightly—vulnerable whiteness;
Love that eluded alleys and implorings
Is pearled in these two oyster-shells of prayer.
"Then adjourn, adjourn," whisper the vespers,

75

"To the farther side of skies.
After the red rose, the red leaf; but
Always somewhere the white love, wooing
You deathward—till your love un-dies."

3.

Different:
Here abstractions have contours; here flesh is wraith;
On these cold and warming stones, only solidity throws no shadow.
And wrists are echoes of the chimes they ring.
(Listen, when the high bells ripple the half-light:
Ideas, ideas, the tall ideas dancing.)
This is Assisi, this is
                    a different love and the same;
What twelve years squandered in boulevards and gropings
Was wine poured for
                    ghosts. You
Will get it back in Umbria tonight.

Assisi, 1945

Charles Against Arno

I. Refrain at the River Charles
II. Etruria

. . .

I. Refrain at the River Charles
(the Harvard Phi Beta Kappa poem of 1953) *

I.

O sunstruck spray, where change and changeless meet:
    I would abscond to the safe silence
    That hides in the heart of the traffic bustle,
    The easy peace of outwardness.
But sun reached down and knit me back to you.
    River I grew from, river I return to,
    I've dredged you for both sun and moon;
    Knew you, I thought, but now what strangeness?
"I will, thou shalt," says Will; "I will, I will";
I want things blue, and I will have them so—
Till every droplet radiates and savors
Blue, blue, and gold. Most fugitive of golds,

---

* At the formal Phi Beta Kappa reading of this poem, it was preceded by the following tentative thematic statement: "The lowest stage is the outer traffic bustle: material flux. The next stage is inner and spiritual but too awake, too willed: view but not vision. The final stage is vision: kept only by not trying to keep it, by not subjecting it to will and daytime wisdom. The sun-drenched spray of the Charles combines into one the two aspects of vision: the ever constant (hinted by sun), the ever changing (hinted by spray)."

    The voice entangled in this poem seems to be somewhat New England, Christian, introspective-symbolic. The contrasting voice, entangled in the subsequent poem "Etruria," seems to be somewhat Mediterranean, older-than-Christian, sensuous-concrete.

Silvering nightly out of tarnished sun.
Once more: blue, blue, and gold! My words are colors,
On which I float all things that do not flow.

But Will rules surfaces and never secrets;
You must escape me till I set you free.

2.

O sunstruck spray, where glow and glacial meet:
       I would abscond to the safe silence
         That hides in the heart of the traffic bustle,
       The cowardice of action, action.
But sun reached down and knit me back to you.
       River I grew from, river I return to,
         I've traced your white and your yellow script;
       Knew you, but now what overwhelming?
Diphthong of tunes outside the brow and in it,
Single pulse of tides that foam both blue and red,
What truth, what prayer, where wave, where blood are one,
Will wake together—clear, clear, one instant clear—
Our ears and you: great unclear voice from sky?

But wakefulness commands not shapes but shadows.
I cannot wake you till you teach me sleep.

3.

O sunstruck spray,
Here the forever and the moment meet.
       I would abscond to the safe silence
         That hides in the heart of the traffic bustle,
       The bland dying of liveliness.
But sun reached down and knit me back to you.
       River I grew from, river I belong to,
         Now circling home to gold from silver:—
       What thunder, O familiar stranger?
Jubilant gold of fabulous ablutions,
Gold undulant on quick wet toy-small hills;
Hammerer at lids; pore-drenching wine of light;

From ripply mirrors upward-falling dew,
Here, here, and hovering, round and round my sight;
And oh what thunder where "flame" and "shout" are one,
Knitting my nerve-strands to your strands of sun.

But sight sees not the vision but the view.
I cannot see you till I doubt my eyes.

II. Etruria

1.

Tamperer vainly tidying up the stream
Of sense-impressions mind can never tie:
The concrete mischief of my Tuscan dust
In your too northern, allegoric eye
Warns that the *stream* is all, the vistas lie.
It drags as earthbound as my pollen must;
It flies as airy as my marble may;
Before you try to think such stream away,
Tamperer, tamperer, fathom noon's own gleam.

2.

The Apennines surround my flat brown tonsure
So vaguely you forget my noon has scissored
More clearly each least shadow of a lizard
Than any silhouette a paper-doll leaves.
The stream is all; each color light can conjure,
Each clasped incitement swells the sensuous stream,
Sonorous as the pattern a chorale leaves—
Yet dust-anointed, never beatific.
Your yearned abstractions cannot live where sol lives;
And even luna's half-lights, clinging, contour
My several greens exultantly specific.
My vines are vines; each tangible full rondure
Is just itself, no symbol and no dream.
That dust is three-dimensional. The olives
Are really there. I am the land I seem.

Sonnet

("*Every day, with statistical regularity, somebody is somewhere or other choosing suicide by drowning in sea water.*")

Through this mild mist I let your hostile spray
Gnash harmless at my shoe, my shin, my knee.
You'll never bark loose, O rhetoric-swollen sea,
From Law whose leash of moonlight tugs your spray.
These foaming, mad-dog lunges of your spray
Affright not man, who sidesteps elegantly
To trick you into docile industry
And flog his engines faster with your spray.

Small numerals muzzle your immensity
And code your passion's meteorology;
You (down, dog, down!) have Law. Are *known*. Man's fluttery
Fidgety wisp of soul alone stays free—
And lawless, law-giving, conquering, armed with the key
To all but itself, breaks daily in your spray.

Love Poem

We are the satraps of a sinking season.
Our year's a Ferris Wheel, whose guests we are.
Before I rise again, I must fall far.

But not with you. Our snow-time aches with treason,

At wheel's deep dip when soil gapes nearest bone.
Then you'll stand up,
                    force doors,
                              fall out alone.

Big Crash Out West

They call streets "boulevards" and build them huge
Where grandpa's ox-cart could not budge;
Here's room for elbows, land of the brave fourth gears.
Speed is the bridge for spanning loneliness.
Until.
            This is the western way to die.
And when the car stops burning, thar he'll lie,
Surrounded by the brothers of his lodge.
O crash for whom their boredoms cry,
Is there—in your sensuous instant—time to guess
At what's unspent, unsensuous years
Never hot with doubt nor faith nor reverence for tears?

Kilroy

(for John H. Finley, Jr.)

(Editor's note: An example of an unfaked epic spirit emerging from the war was the expression "Kilroy was here," scribbled everywhere by American soldiers and implying that nothing was too adventurous or remote.)

I.

Also Ulysses once—that other war.
        (Is it because we find his scrawl

Today on every privy door
That we forget his ancient rôle?)
Also was there—he did it for the wages—
When a Cathay-drunk Genoese set sail.
Whenever "longen folk to goon on pilgrimages,"
Kilroy is there;
        he tells The Miller's Tale.

2.

At times he seems a paranoiac king
Who stamps his crest on walls and says, "My own!"
But in the end he fades like a lost tune,
Tossed here and there, whom all the breezes sing.
"Kilroy was here"; these words sound wanly gay,
        Haughty yet tired with long marching.
He is Orestes—guilty of what crime?—
        For whom the Furies still are searching;
        When they arrive, they find their prey
(Leaving his name to mock them) went away.
Sometimes he does not flee from them in time:
"Kilroy was—"
        (with his blood a dying man
        Wrote half the phrase out in Bataan.)

3.

Kilroy, beware. "HOME" is the final trap
That lurks for you in many a wily shape:
In pipe-and-slippers plus a Loyal Hound
        Or fooling around, just fooling around.
Kind to the old (their warm Penelope)
But fierce to boys,
        thus "home" becomes that sea,
Horribly disguised, where you were always drowned,—
        (How could suburban Crete condone
The yarns you would have V-mailed from the sun?)—
And folksy fishes sip Icarian tea.

One stab of hopeless wings imprinted your
             Exultant Kilroy-signature
Upon sheer sky for all the world to stare:
                "I was there! I was there! I was there!"

4.

God is like Kilroy; He, too, sees it all;
That's how He knows of every sparrow's fall;
That's why we prayed each time the tightropes cracked
On which our loveliest clowns contrived their act.
The G. I. Faustus who was
                              everywhere
Strolled home again. "What was it like outside?"
Asked Can't, with his good neighbors Ought and But
And pale Perhaps and grave-eyed Better Not;
For "Kilroy" means: the world is very wide.
          He was there, he was there, he was there!

And in the suburbs Can't sat down and cried.

The Blind Doge at 83 *

Venice arose: a mist of steel, a patience
Of sea-walls, merely gray to fear's dilating
Mere outward eyes, yet purplest-cored of towns.

But guilty purple. Like such blood as day shuns,
Such ill-spilt blood as nightly jolts (cascading
Up palace-steps) the sleep of ill-won crowns.

* Fourth Crusade, 1202–04: under pretext of crusading against the Moslems,
Enrico Dandolo, the octogenarian blind Doge, blasphemously outwitted both
Pope and Emperor by instead conquering the Eastern Roman Empire with
the Venetian navy.

Enrico Dandolo came celebrating
His eighty-third year, vowing: "I renounce—
Being blind, bent, nine-tenths dead—renunciations."

Enrico Dandolo came un-Crusading,
His wrinkles lordlier than decorations,
His smiling deadlier than judges' frowns.

His dry-veined aspen-hands—(more devastating
Than if the very flood-tide would pronounce
Declaration of war upon the Grecian stations)—

Pounded rough Adriatic inundations
Down on the suave Aegean's tired waiting.
Cursed with last breath by every Greek who drowns,

He shook a Caesar's empire like a plaything.
Only his will—old warship of the passions—
Lived on; and wore his limbs as limbs wear gowns;

And peeled past triumphs off like frills of clowns;
And forced, with pirate-grin, a prouder mating,
Sheathed in the Rome of all the eastern nations.

Brushing the loot and flute-girls of the Asians
Aside like side-whirls when the big waves pounce,
Through eighty bad years never vacillating,

The blind one stomped into Byzantium.

For an Assyrian Frieze

"The city Aridi I besieged and captured. I erected a pyramid of heads in front of this city. Its young men and women I burned in a bonfire. I built a life-size statue of myself. To Arzashku, the royal city of Arramu, I advanced. In the strength of my manhood, like a wild bull, I trampled his land into ruins. Arzashku I destroyed, devastated, and burned with fire. I erected pyramids of heads in front of this city. Others I impaled on stakes. I built a large statue of my royalty."

—inscription of 850 B.C.

"I, the great king, the powerful king, king of the world, King of Assyria, the king whose path was a cyclone, whose battle was a flaming sea, I am powerful, all-powerful, exalted, almighty, majestic, all-important in power."

—inscription of 870 B.C.

Sometimes a lion with a prophet's beard
Lopes from a bas-relief to stretch his claws.
His bestial eyes are wonderfully sad.

Then he grows wings, the terrible king grows wings,
And flies above the black Euphrates loam,
Hunting for enemies of Nineveh.

His names are Shamshi and Adádnirari,
Tiglath-Piléser, Assurbanipal,
And the first Sargon of Dur-Shárukin.

"The day my chariots stormed the town, I waxed
My beard with oil of rose and waterlily,
And freed nine pearl-caged nightingales, and built

85

A pillar of skulls so high it stabbed the sun."
(Was that the tomb's voice, or the desert-wind's?
Or ours? What ghost is still our roaring priest?)

The scribes shall say: his will outflew his wisdom.
The saints shall say: his was the sin of pride.
The skulls say nothing. And the lizards grin.

This is the rapture that the Gentiles feared
When Joshua made music masterful.
Each sinew is a harp-string crouched to twang.

The treble of such bloodlust if he pounced
Would shriek an anti-social kind of beauty
Like parrots at a pirate massacre.

Then back to stone. In stone he sleeps the least.
It's not with love his brooding glitters so.
Earth spawns no gangrene half so luminous

As the contagion of those molten eyes.

Tug of War

Upon the rough earth resting,
Mind backward grows toward boys
Who wonder at distant blasting
Through louder tinkle of toys.

The day a soldier flinches,
Mind younger grows toward years
Where sandpiles blur with trenches,
Bad wolves with bombardiers.

Across barbed wire dangling,
Will ever hands unmesh

Two things not meant for tangling,
This metal and this flesh?

It's all a crisscross game now,
Each with the toy he lacks.
It's madmen love the Lamb now.
Mary hones the axe.

(*1967 version*)

6: Persimmons

"The character of the 'mysterious, smiling, heartless Stranger' [in Euripides, *The Bacchae*] who came out of the East, disquiets the mind with its irreconcilable qualities of beauty and guile. His power is equally ambiguous; it seems to be divine in some of its manifestations, fiendishly malignant in others, and the shadow of imposture falls upon some. Pentheus called him 'a foreign wizard skilled in spells'; he may have been nothing more than that; but he controlled the Bacchantes absolutely, he sent all the women of Thebes to rave and dance upon the hills, and he had the still more perilous gift of self-intoxication."

—E. M. BUTLER, *The Myth of the Magus*
Cambridge University Press,
New York: 1948

The Persimmon Tree

Not as we wish, accoutred regal,
Our soarers land but pent in cloud.
So must we take each molted eagle
Just as he comes or do without.
No radiance radiates. Its birth is
Dark-stained with lusts and blasphemies.
We sing them shiny if we please.
Or snuff them. Either way, unclean.
We dodge with outrage or derision
Truths that assault us squashily:
Each clowning, sweetish, harsh-cored vision
That shoots from the persimmon tree.
Brief bloom, we always wrong you; earth is
A drabber patch than need have been.

Poet

"Toute forme créée, même par l'homme, est
immortelle. Car la forme est indépendante
de la matière, et ce ne sont pas les
molécules qui constituent la forme."
—(Baudelaire, *Mon Coeur Mis à Nu*)

1.

The night he died, earth's images all came
To gloat in liberation round his tomb.

Now vengeful colors, stones, and faces dare
    To argue with his metaphor;
And stars his fancy painted on the skies
Drop down like swords
                    to pierce his too wide eyes.

2.

Words that begged favor at his court in vain—
Lush adverbs, senile rhymes in tattered gowns—
    Send notes to certain exiled nouns
And mutter openly against his reign.
While rouged clichés hang out red lights again,
Hoarse refugees report from far-flung towns
That exclamation-marks are running wild
And prowling half-truths carried off a child.

3.

But he lives on in form, and form shall shatter
    This tuneless mutiny of matter.
His bones are dead; his voice is horribly strong.
Those famed vibrations of life's dancing dust,
Whose thrice-named pangs are "birth" and "death" and "lust,"
Are but the spilt iambics of his song.
Scansion of flesh in endless ebb and flow,
The drums of duty and renown's great gong—
Mere grace-notes of that living thousand-year
Tyrannic metronome whose every gear
Is some shy craftsman buried long ago.
What terror crowns the sweetness of all song?

4.

What hardness leaps at us from each soft tune
And hammers us to shapes we never planned?
This was a different dying from our own.
    Call every wizard in the land—
Bell, book, and test tube; let the dark be rife
With every exorcism we command.
In vain. This death is stronger than our life.

92

In vain we drive our stakes through such a haunter
Or woo with spiced applaudings such a heart.
His news of April do but mock our winter
Like maps of heaven breathed on window-frost
By cruel clowns in codes whose key is lost.
Yet some sereneness in our rage has guessed
That we are being blessed and blessed and blessed
When least we know it and when coldest art
    Seems hostile,
        useless,
            or apart.

6.

Not worms, not worms in such a skull
But rhythms, rhythms writhe and sting and crawl.
He sings the seasons round from bud to snow.
And all things are because he willed them so.

Decorum and Terror: Homage to Goethe and Hart Crane

The "siren of the springs of guilty song"
Is not the muse of Weimar's hushed salon.
(Jazz bands would make Frau von Stein hysteric.)

Conversely, *Faust Part Two*, though bumpy, jars
No spindrift off the beers in Brooklyn bars.
(Classic discs would give a gob an earache.)

Yet you need each other, mint and thyme,
Yours the cool and yours the acrid clime;
Art's two equal, different truths you mime.
Since a ghost can vault the fence of time,

Meet as house-guests here within my rhyme.
(Distant first, each cagey and satiric.)

As ice breeds bears, polarity brings strife:
'I hate you, Johann, for your Tory life.'
—'Bohemia's old reproach to poise Homeric.'

'But that same poise with cant and cushions rife
(Official titles, prizes, buffer-wife)
Appeases Babbitts—while I feel their knife.
Old fraud, your crass success makes me choleric.'

Then Johann: 'Banal scars from burgher-baiting
Are not the only pangs of song-creating.
You chose the doom that cancels woes Wertheric,
But I—I lived them. Whose the grimmer sea-wreck?'
—'Woes neat and brain-planned as a labeled key-rack
You made vast myths of, hamming like a Garrick.'

'And was your Bridge myth any less chimeric?
Walt, city slicker, sold the unaware hick
Not even gold-bricks—bricks of rusty ferric.
(Who lacks wings to lift him, builds a derrick.)'

'Your German Welt-schmalz I, in turn, admonish;
Eke *grands amours* from tussles in a hay-rick
Or "soulful" moods from pressures atmospheric,
But one thing spare us: call them not "*daemonisch*"—
While buttering patrons, unctious as a cleric.'

'Patrons? Before you snub the courtier's prance,
Explain a certain check of Otto Kahn's.
Amerika, du hast es besser in finance:
Have you no agent, Hart, by any chance,
To book my lectures? Here's my song and dance:
For women's clubs, the Elder Statesman stance;
For eggheads, *Faust* translated in Amharic.
My fees would burst all boundaries numeric.
You, too, thinned Sapphic gold of pure romance
With pompous public dross of odes Pindaric.'

'When I marched terror through decorum's barrack,
Or you your Werther through salons Weimaric,
In all art's wars no triumph was more Pyrrhic.'
—'Wars you yourself, your own worst mutineer, wreck.'

'Better a war well lost and meteoric
Than triumphs basking drowsy and euphoric.
Johann, your ego never shared or co-starred;
Your secret fear of failing makes you boast hard.
Your classicism? What a corny postcard,
An alp all scenic'd up and bella-vista'd.'
—'Don't try to act as earthy as a coastguard;
You're not exactly hearty and two-fisted.
Americana lures you, Hart—resist it.
There's nothing wrong with being tender-wristed;
Your gift is more Athenian than Doric;
Your best songs are not ruggedly folkloric
Nor grossly and gregariously choric
But subtly—this I honor—esoteric.'

'I honor you for being self-invented.
Not even Jenghiz Khan was more Tartaric
Than you toward your own flesh, O self-tormented;
Chisel in hand, from your own myth you dented
All frailty away before they missed it.
The bust looks grand but never yet existed.
Johann, your history is unhistoric.'

'Your ways of seeing earth are untelluric;
Hart Crane, your necromancy smells sulphuric.
Not even Dracula was more vampiric
Than you on your own nerves: immensities
Of visual tropes from verbal densities,
An elephantiasis of imageries.
Fool when literal, genius when metaphoric.'

Then Hart: 'You, too, were once not allegoric
But blazed with passions sizzlingly phosphoric.
You now praise calm because can raise no storm.'

95

At once, through blinds, a schoolgirl's giggles swarm.
Ulriké enters—ancient blood beats warm—
Art's last conformist leaps to nonconform.

Dawn follows, catapulting ghosts to flight.
And two great artists, wranglers half the night,
Departing find each other strangely right:
You the classic, you the new-world lyric.
(Homage to both your shrines from Peter Viereck.)

An Owl for a Nightingale

1.

One tawny paw is all it takes to squash
This owl who nests in brows his grounded stare.
And I am both what anchors and what flies,
The sheltering eyelids and the straining eyes.
What ailed me from the arsenals of shape
To wear so armorless a pilgrim's-cape?
And who am, who is "I"? If soul, I'd flash
Through this poor pelt—through, off, no matter where,
Just to wrench free one instant. Or else I'd shout
In midnight ululations—"let me out"—
          Straight up at Such as cooped me here:
"How did you get me into such a scrape?"

2.

But "I" being less than soul, of dustier plume:
If I escape, it is myself I lose.
Big hooting flapping earth-bound ego, close
Your hopeless wings at last and bless aloud—
Seeing only song flits through—this slandered home,
This warm sweet roost built from such stinking trash.

Sing out its theme (there never was but one),
Throw back your head and sing it all again,
Sing the bewildered honor of the flesh.
I say the honor of our flesh is love;
I say no soul, no god could love as we—
A forepaw stalking us from every cloud—
Who loved while sentenced to mortality.
        Never to be won by shield, love fell
O only to the wholly vulnerable.

3.

What hubbub rocks the nest? What panic-freighted
Invasion—when he tried to sing—dilated
The big eyes of my blinking, hooting fowl?
A cartilaginous, most rheumatic squeak
Portends (half mocks) the change; the wrenched bones creak;
Unself descends, invoked or uninvited;
Self ousts itself, consumed and consummated;
An inward-facing mask is what must break.
The magic feverish fun of chirping, all
That professorial squints and squawks indicted,
Is here—descends, descends—till wisdom, hoarse
From bawling beauty out, at last adores,
Possessed by metamorphosis so strong.
Then, with a final flutter, philomel—
How mud-splashed, what a mangy miracle!—
Writhes out of owl and stands with drooping wing.
Just stands there. Moulted, naked, two-thirds dead.
From shock and pain (and dread of holy dread)
        Suddenly vomiting.
Look away fast, you are watching the birth of song.

                                    (*1964 version*)

Dolce Ossessione

Will no one watch me? Look, I'll dance on thread
Or hold my breath for cameras till I burst.
Step close, please; see, I'll pick your pockets first
And shine—like truth? like lies?—and then drop dead.
Pathfinder, poacher, voodoo god, and quack:
My names, unending as an almanac,
Spin round me like a madman's spelling-bee.
I am the prodigal who won't come back;

Phobic of wheels, I'll hide beneath the sea.

The sea! What beast existences I'll choose!
At first I'll curl in wombs of shells and doze
For years and years in tepid, crooning dark.
I'll urge obsession on: an eel, I'll swim
To every far Sargasso of my whim.
When I hear bathers laugh, I'll be a shark.

A flame-scaled trout, I'll shimmer through your nets—
Like lies? like truth?—and gasp on fatal sands.
Trailed fawning by lascivious lean-ribbed cats,
What child will scoop me up,
                                        what pudgy hands?

Ballad of the Jollie Gleeman

(A parable for songcraft—or haplie politicke)

High thanes and highborn ladies, stay and heed
An ambling gleeman sore athirst for mead.

I chaunt a rime whose end will stound you all;
On sward nor sea, its like ye'll never hear.
No overweener I but tuneful thrall,
A lackpelf glad to babble for his beer.

(*tuneth cithern and commenceth; bawcocks and damoizels daunce winsomelie together*)

A dragon-worm did bogey all the East.
From pilgrims plump he gat him bonnie feast.
He wrake his wrath on them, atop a wrack
Of saunterers who sauntered never back.
He gouged, he gored, he thwarted every thwack.
Atop twelve skulls did smirk yon shameless Beast.

A pure Crusader, pricking to Seint Terre,
Did meet yon godless worm, flesh-gorging there.
With splendid spleen our hero's eyën shone;
He clave that worm unto the neckë-bone;
He drave his swingle till it swisht the air.
Hell's henchman wallopt he in his own lair.

(*poureth self jug of mead and quaffeth*)

Pax bless such sword-playe, bless Seint George's dreame!
Pox blight them all that playe not on God's teame!
Scathers and skulkers, doers in the dark,
Each werewolf (grislie guest with baleful bark),
Each Thing that poppeth out from under stones:
Grace graunt them all such sore-nickt neckë-bones.

(*shuddereth righteouslie; damoizels, while dauncing wantonlie, make sign of true cross with their fans*)

Out tript a princess, blanche as moonës dew,
Imprisond in yon dragon's swart purlieu.
More sheen her tress than Troytown ever knew;
More sheer her dress than spider's treachrous fleece,
Thro which did beck and keek her dimplie knees.
Her paps were pippins such as Eden grew

To Adam's bane whan did befall that Fall
From which disgrace may Grace redeeme us all.
(Withouten Grace no soul is tuppence worth,
As hell-folk wot; their groans give pleasaunt mirth
To gentle Seints above.) For love of Grace
Our hero holp yon helpless love-ripe lass.

*(wipeth brow and eke filleth new jug; courtiers toss him coins
and yawn)*

For love of her, he dropt both shield and sword.
(To breach sic maidenhead were goodlie sport.)
With dapper dirk she breached our hero's side;
"Quaint thanks thou gavest me," he sulkt—and died.
But she—"sweet Fiend, sweet ghastlie worm!" she cried.
(Praise Grace, whose ways we ken not, but record.)

In pain her loathlie lord his claws did flail.
Soft swaddled she his sore-nickt neckë-bone
And, crooning, nurst her dank dark leman hale;
Then, hand in paw, they clomb his ancient throne.
Atop such pile of skulls as sought the Grail,
Beautie and Beast once more made amorous moan.

*(unstringeth cithern and draineth jug; then bolteth shut gate while
bowing reverentlie)*

Now is yon arch-worm Earl of all the East.
So droll a tale, I ween ye never wist.
Ye've had your song, and I—I'll have my feast
(removeth jollie mask and revealeth monstrous jaws)
On all of you. Yon Fiend whereof I sing
(groweth mountain-high)
Is your poor bard. Too late to scape my fang.
Now, daintie lordlings, daunce your final fling.

1946

Photomontage of the Urban Parks

Though birds can flee when colors scorch like embers,
The lawns lie trapped below in fire and frost and dark.
Image of love in all love's fierce Novembers:
A burning oak-leaf in a shivering park.

But even in cities: Pan. Or was it Francis?
Then parks, all parks, lunge free and flood our eyes.
Vengeful return of disestablished fancies:
A live kaleidoscope of fireflies.

Birds are exploding into bloom and glowing,
And petals fan our sleep with little wings.
(Into your eardrum what glass snake is flowing?
It is a Moorish fountain, and it sings.)

Stalactites raping soft moss grottoes. Shouting
Ducks from Bronx Park on Oxford swan-ponds floating.
Versailles and Schoenbrunn, waltzing knee to knee,
Elope into the eighteenth century.

All spins and mixes. Who cried, "Stop!"? Alarms
Won't help now. Faster. Whirlwind, whirl again
A park called Eden, Francis *with* Saint Pan,
The white snow with the rainbow in her arms.

1946

Small Perfect Manhattan

Unable to breathe, I inhaled the classic Aegean.
Losing my northern shadow, I sheared the noon
    Of an almond grove. The tears of marble
        Thanked me for laughter.

Shapes! And "Release, release" rustled the quarries;
"One touch will free the serenity locked in our stones."
    But archipelagoes of olives
        Distracted me shorewards,

Where sails were ripening toward an African sleep.
This south wind was no friend of the wind of harps.
    Not destiny but destination
        Incited the grain-ships.

"Nevertheless be of cheer," said a jolly skipper;
"I sell sick goats that once were deft at flutes.
    The lizard who now is proconsul of Carthage
        Will bury you sweetly."

Then No to sweet Charon. Then home—then not to Sahara,
The elephants'-graveyard of classics—ascended the singing
    Green I wove just the size of the brow of
        Small perfect Manhattan.

Athens, 1949

7 : Cradle Songs and Elegies

"*We natives always say: 'You just can't miss it,'*
Not even if you shut your eyes."

—*page 109*

Proöimion

Evil and Easter steer this star, rash babe.
Foul fellow He who dolve so strait a glebe.
Fey fellow He who died for such daft globe.
Woe worth the mime who be thy astrolabe.

Though woxe a wight so stout as oaken wood,
Sware he by Mahound—or by Godis rood,
Cowl-clad—or clipt more doxies than he wed,
Him felled swart axman that more stoutly hewed.
     ... Ho Carpenter! wilt mend our smitten wood?

Newcomer, reck no rede but this, perfay:
Thy masque below hight "Love and Wellaway"
(Certës, withouten both were nary play).
Then strut thy buskins; sigh but strut them gay.

Boy, stand too proud for chapmen when they prate.
(Or carl or younker, equally askew.)
'Tis mummers, mummers do delight Jesú.
Only the gleeman glegly ogles fate.

Foul fellow lispeth sweet but drinketh gore.
Fey fellow He who drank vile vinegar;
For love of thee, He gat Him thorny gear;
He gat scant dayspring for the dawn He bare.

Twain fellows have and halve the soul of thee;
Sic bane and boon hath each nativity.
Furies and nurses trim each fledgling-tree.
And I: as mime.
            And in thy pate all three.

Six Theological Cradle Songs *

1. Better Come Quietly

Baby John: O kinsfolk and gentlefolk, PLEASE be forgiving,
    But nothing can lure me to living, to living.
    I'm snug where I am; I don't WISH to burst through.
Chorus of Nurses, Furies, & Muses:
    That's what YOU think. If only you KNEW.

Baby John: Well then YES, I'll be BORN, but my EARTH will be heaven;
    My dice will throw nothing but seven-eleven;
    Life is tall lilacs, all giddy with dew.
Chorus of Nurses, Furies, & Muses:
    That's what YOU think. If only you KNEW.

Baby John: Well then YES, there'll be sorrows, be sorrows that best me;
    But these are mere teasings to test me, to test me.
    We'll ZOOM from our graves when God orders us to.
Chorus of Nurses, Furies, & Muses:
    That's what YOU think. If only you KNEW.

Baby John: Well then YES, I'll belie my belief in survival.
    But IF there's no God, then at least there's no devil:
    If at LAST I must die—well, at LEAST when I do,
    It's clear I won't sizzle.
Chorus of Nurses, Furies, & Muses:
       If only you KNEW.

---

* Composed for my son's christening, 1946. The capitalizations, in songs
1 and 6, imitate the bounce and emphasis of a child chanting while stamp-
ing on the springs of his crib.

2. Why Can't I Live Forever?

'Here comes a candle to light you to bed,
And here comes a chopper to chop off your head.'
—Nursery rhyme

Death is a blind flamingo, hunting fishes.
He does not mean to gobble you or me—
And when his beak swings wildly, never wishes
To scare us so. If only he could see.

At night he wades through surf to seek a mate.
That's why he stinks of salt and oyster shells.
It is his blindness keeps him celibate;
This bungler thinks he kisses when he kills.

I wish he wouldn't make us die. I wish
He'd spread his wings one night and fly away
To higher planets for his girls and fish.
But he's got used to earth
                                      and plans to stay.

3. Game Called on Account of Darkness

Once there was a friend.
He watched me from the sky.
Maybe he never lived at all.
Maybe too much friendship made him die.

When the gang played cops-and-robbers in the alley,
It was my friend who told me which were which.
Now he doesn't tell me any more.
(Which team am I playing for?)

My science teacher built a telescope
To show me every answer in the end.
I stared and stared at every star for hours.

I couldn't find my friend.

At Sunday school they said I breathe too much.
When I hold my breath within the under
Side of earth, they said I'll find my friend.
. . . I wonder.

He was like a kind of central-heating
In our big cold house, and that was good.
One by one I have to chop my toys now,
As firewood.

Every time I stood upon a crossroads,
It made me mad to feel him watch me choose.
I'm glad there's no more spying while I play.
Still, I'm sad he went away.

4. Blindman's Buff

Night-watchmen think of dawn and things auroral.
Clerks wistful for Bermudas think of coral.
The poet in New York still thinks of laurel.
(But lovers think of death and touch each other
As if to prove that love is still alive.)

The Martian space-crew, in an earthward dive,
Think of their sweet unearthly earth Up There,
Where darling monsters romp in airless air.
(Two lovers think of death and touch each other,
Fearing the day when only one's alive.)

We think of cash, but cash does not arrive.
We think of fun, but fate will not connive.
We never mention death. Do we survive?
(The lovers think of death and touch each other
To live their love while love is yet alive.)

Prize-winners are so avid when they strive;
They race so far; they pile their toys so high.
Only a cad would trip them. Yet they die.

(The lovers think of death and touch each other;
Of all who live, these are the most alive.)

When all the lemming-realists contrive
To swim—where to?—in life's enticing tide,
Only a fool would stop and wait outside.
(The lovers stop and wait and touch each other.
Who twinly think of death are twice alive.)

Plump creatures smack their lips and think they thrive;
The hibernating bear, but half alive,
Dreams of free honey in a stingless hive.
He thinks of life at every lifeless breath.
(The lovers think of death.)

5. The New Guest Promenades with a Feather in His Cap

"That sunset tourists hike so far to visit,
Where shall I trail it and how recognize?"
> *The famous view that's viewing you is ice.*

"I'll toss you all the tips your palms solicit.
Which way?"
> *Young master, anywhere you wish it.*
> *You'll need no alpenstock. Your cab—dismiss it.*
> *Only your skin, sir; try it on for size.*

"Guide, stop the sun, please. And be more explicit.
I run and run; the sunset faster flies."
> *You'll sleep with it the night you catch and kiss it.*
> *But what's the hurry? Waiting will suffice:*
> *Say, sixty years ... then any bait will fish it.*

"Come, fellow, come; show me that paradise."
> *Your heels will see it if you scan the skies.*

"Old fool, what Baedeker can I elicit,
Which final inn to answer my where-is-it?"
> *We natives always say: 'You just can't miss it,'*
> *Not even if you shut your eyes.*

6. Hide and Seek

(an Easter ballad)

"Come OUT, come OUT, wherEVer you are,"
The frisking children chorused.
   When playtime ends,
   All hidden friends
Are bound to come out of the forest.

"Come OUT, come OUT, wherEVer you are,"
The tidy children chorused.
   In the short proud street
   Where our lives are neat
On the nearer side of the forest.

"Come OUT, come OUT, wherEVer you are,"
The puzzled children chorused.
   When fun is over,
   Why doesn't the rover
Come whooping out of the forest?

"Come OUT, come OUT, wherEVer you are,"
The lonely children chorused;
   For the greater the dark
   The less the lark
When you wait till dusk near a forest.

"Come OUT, come OUT, wherEVer you are,"
The shivering children chorused.
   With some wonderful toy
   Can we hold back the boy
Who is westering into the forest?

"Come OUT, come OUT, wherEVer you are,"
We aging children chorused—
   While beyond our shout
   A boy comes out
On the farther side of the forest.

Six Elegies

1. *Vale* from Carthage

(for my brother, 1944)

I, now at Carthage. He, shot dead at Rome.
Shipmates last May. "And what if one of us,"
I asked last May, in fun, in gentleness,
"Wears doom, like dungarees, and doesn't know?"
He laughed, *"Not see Times Square again?"* The foam,
Feathering across that deck a year ago,
Swept those five words—like seeds—beyond the seas
    Into his future. There they grew like trees;
      And as he passed them there next spring, they laid
    Upon his road of fire their sudden shade.
Though he had always scraped his mess-kit pure
And scrubbed redeemingly his barracks floor,
Though all his buttons glowed their ritual-hymn
Like cloudless moons to intercede for him,
No furlough fluttered from the sky. He will
Not see Times Square—he will not see—he will
Not see Times
        change; at Carthage (while my friend,
Living those words at Rome, screamed in the end)
I saw an ancient Roman's tomb and read
"Vale" in stone. Here two wars mix their dead:
    Roman, my shipmate's dream walks hand in hand
      With yours tonight ("New York again" and "Rome"),
    Like widowed sisters bearing water home
    On tired heads through hot Tunisian sand
    In good cool urns, and says, "I understand."

Roman, you'll see your Forum Square no more;
What's left but this to say of any war?

2. Benediction

(for a father)

When the first vague years, the years of questions and toys,
Resolved into years of the boy with his nose in old fable,
    It was good to hear a father's voice
    Across the lull of the breakfast table.
When the second fate, the years of answer and choice,
Diffused into years of the youth on the parapet,
    Where maps went rainbowing round such tallness
    In outspread valleys of my whim,
Then earth was good in multicolored allness,
And I loved all of it. But loved not him.

The third fate ambushed. Then the three roads met;
I faced the enemy the Sphinx foretold.
Again, again the ancient rites unfold.
Must all men play out fables to the end?
    Are men themselves not fates?—to bend
Their chains to rungs? I will outbless that curse,
I praise alike the young years and the old:
The enemy the Sphinx foretold, I slew;
    That, too, was good—forgive my doubt, my smallness—
It all is good, it all is good, him I loved too.

3. Killed by a Car at 21

(to George F. Delacorte)

A breath of awareness in water, fire, and earth,
More than machine by one breath, was how you began.

And in time were a poet, were my friend, from birth
Anti-metallic; while we rode, you ran.
You were rooted to first things, sea and land and fire;
Not to computers. Not you, when pricked, would bleed
Machine oil. Bleeding was for keeps. The reed
Of Pascal: "Mountain, crush me if you can."
Your life was a race against wheels ("unmechanize man")
And wondered beyond them: to prove speed is slow in the end.
Then wheels laid a plot against roots and struck higher.

That's all: you were a poet and my friend;
A car passed; now you are water, earth, and fire.

1939

4. Grace of Pine

(Dallas, 1963)

1.

November is the summer season
(Gun-sight sun-light twine)
On November twenty-second
As the southwest year is reckoned
Roses shine.

.   .   .

Sunless Boston roseless Georgetown
(Was ever Cape Cod green?)
On November twenty-second
As the northern year is reckoned
Fall thuds between.

2.

See a horse without a rider
Hear three shots a thud of pine
Nation-welding twenty-second
When whole continents are reckoned

Climates twine.

. . .

Now the old outlive the young
Twine the seasons fall is green
Shiver sunny twenty-second
Pine is red a young Spring beckoned
Glaciers rise between.

3.

But the heart has heart's own landscape
Inner grace of pine
Sands that only blood makes fecund
Ice that tears melt in a second
(Death-pang birth-pang twine).

. . .

Dust-words clashing deserts wrangling
Only "style" stayed green
(Magic no machine has reckoned)
Not those slogans was what beckoned
But that grace between.

4.

Shots transfix but shots transfigure
Darken but outshine
Let November twenty-second
Be three shocks through years unreckoned
Crest
      root
            wreath of pine:—

. . .

Crest
      outshine the tribal beacons
Root
      entwine between
Wreathe black rose and white (a second
Lincoln agony has beckoned)
Catalytic evergreen.

5. Hexameters, Pentameters

(for her)

I

Too tuned to your personal rhythm on stairways, I lose for your sake
Everything else in the world into overtones, all out of reach.
Because, when tired, your forehead is earnest as children at play
Many a garden ago, your shoulders many shrugs older,
Therefore I memorize wildly the face I see, outside and in,
Each ray-like eyelash skirting some afterglow long out of reach.
So does sky's afterglow drag out of reach on hilltops
Frayed rays of party-skirts, girl's flounce of purple. No,
Already gray.

2.

Shadow of cheekbones, clouded slant of cheeks
I see but not the skeleton beneath
That lovers hymn in banal bitterness.
If I unveil that face-veiled future also,
Then what I see is this: not skull but urn.
A quick light flounce of ashes out of reach,
Is this the dusty hem of the last trailing
Of party-skirts, a moment's purple? No,
Already gray.

6. Which of Us Two?

When both are strong with tenderness, too wild
With oneness to be severance-reconciled;
When even the touch of fingertips can shock
Both to such seesaw mutuality
Of hot-pressed opposites as smelts a tree
Tighter to its dryad than to its own tight bark;
When neither jokes or mopes or hates alone
Or wakes untangled from the other; when

More-warm-than-soul, more-deep-than-flesh are one
In marriage of the very skeleton;—

When, then, death peels mere flesh off half this love
And locks it from the unstripped half above,
Who's ever sure which side of soil he's on?
Have I lain seconds here, or years like this?
I'm sure of nothing else but loneliness
And darkness. Here's such black as stuffs a tomb,
Or merely midnight in an unshared room.
Holding my breath for fear my breath is gone,
Unmoving and afraid to try to move,
Knowing only you have somehow left my side,

I lie here, wondering which of us has died.

8: Grotesques

"I'll honor gaucheness anywhere I find it
And the deep sadness of a shaggy hope."

—*page 125*

To a Sinister Potato

O vast earth-apple, waiting to be fried,
Of all the starers the most many-eyed,
What furtive purpose hatched you long ago
In Indiana or in Idaho?

In Indiana and in Idaho
Snug underground, the great potatoes grow,
Puffed up with secret paranoias unguessed
By all the duped and starch-fed Middle West.

Like coiled-up springs or like a will-to-power
The fat and earthy lurkers bide their hour,
The silent watchers of our raucous show
In Indiana or in Idaho.

"They deem us dull, a food and not a flower.
Wait! We'll outshine all roses in our hour.
Not wholesomeness but mania swells us so
In Indiana and in Idaho.

"In each Kiwanis Club on every plate
So bland and health-exuding do we wait
That Indiana never, never knows
How much we envy stars and hate the rose."

Some doom will strike (as all potatoes know)
When—once too often mashed in Idaho—
From its cocoon the drabbest of earth's powers
Rises and is a star.
     And shines.
     And lours.

1945

The Orphan Monologue

(buried self of the Oliver Twist tribe)

1.

Life reaches out. Needs necklaces to drag on,
Linking and linked. Then how can life be this:
No string, no beads but island emptiness?
Your kindness keep. Use it to grease a sow
Or sink a shaft in it to oil your station wagon.
The last kind sir who served me prayer to gag on
Coddles four stitches at his cheekbone now.
Mature talk, too—unbitter, balanced right—
Poise it as canapé on bric-a-brac.
I can report about quicksand. Who of your pack
Knows what embrace means? Only drowners hold tight.

2.

We need: we seize. Shadowless on earth,
Poachers of the fading light
Of all old cities, we shiver backwards toward birth.
Our treks become your highways; heels have scrawled
The nomad epic of the parentless.
We hunt the two intensities we lack,
The warm one and the hotter sunless one:
Not love alone—
Even our hate their death forestalled.
Although the highways of the Western dusk are glad
With an old Theban ambiguity tonight,
That knife-thrust—where the three roads bless—
No orphan savors. I want my birthright back.
I want to hate the father I never had.

Ennui

("death by glacier . . . one body still missing")

Trapped me in ice. No, not one chink is gaping.
How many eons now before I melt?
I wait the shattering kiss the sun withheld
And long to join the free and jumping dead.
My walls turn all things blue, through which I see
Blue generations born and die, escaping
In happy twirling ghost-swarms, all but me,
The only ghost on earth with wings unspread.

Outside, my bodiless sisters frisk and dive.
I'd show them speed, could I but get away.
Alas, alas, the snows that froze me dead
Have sealed me in my old lugubrious clay,
The only ghost on earth who isn't gay.
When I consider all that waits ahead
(Years, years of boredom in my icy bed,
No books to read and not one game to play),

Sometimes I almost wish I were alive.

Homily on the Piety of All Herd Animals

(an urban pastoral)

I.

You pilgrims of the Rural Myth who flee
New York
          come home, come home again, and see

What pastoral still soothes the age of smoke:
Theocritus now hymns a metal flock—

"Fifth Avenue Buses," iron-skinned yet mild
(Tame fire-puffers who would not singe a child),
Cowering low-roofed calves and towering bulls,
Grazing technology's Arcadian hills.

2.

As some lost troll might stumble on the lair
Of sleeping dragons
                        and might stare and stare
And marvel that their snores made mountains shake
And run away on tiptoe lest they wake,

So now by chance I find the warehouse sheds
Where tired buses doze in secret beds,
From all New York as artfully concealed
As elephant graveyards in the Congo weald.

3.

You sleep! May muses bless each dreaming wheel,
Rhymed quatrains of Manhattan's song-in-steel,
And bless your fenders, staunch as tusks in rage,
Heroic couplets
                    on an asphalt page.

O noble brutes whose honor is: "We serve,"
Your crooning engines nurse our every nerve
With patient, gawky love through urban stress.
Such heavy ever-bungled kindliness

Implies not sleekness but sheer shagginess:
Riderless once in your young ice-age time,
MAMMOTHS,
                turned equine for a single dime.

4.

More chivalrous than subways and more silent,

Green double-decker landmarks of our island,
Big loyal lopers, through our smog and rain
You lumber out
              in pious herds
                       each dawn,

Then scatter far on separate lonely treks,
Then here at midnight huddle flank to flank.
And now you sleep! Lest rusty squeaks should vex
Your well-earned peace, may every spring relax;

May gulps and gulps of oil bless every thirsty tank.

Love Song to Eohippus

Dictionary definition: "Eohippus, Greek for dawn-horse, small grace-
ful prehistoric ancestor of modern equine family; size of rabbit; had
four toes, no hoofs."

1.

Dance, dance in this museum case,
Ballet-star of our mammal race,
You first shy avatar of grace.

2.

Sweet Eohippus, "dawn-horse" in
    That golden Attic tongue which now
        Like you and Helen is extinct,
Like Cheshire cat of fading grin,
    Like Carthage and like Villon's snow,
        With death and beauty gently linked.

3.

Yet all are deathless in their fashion:

You live in science, they in song,
    You in museums, she in Homer.
She cannot help but live while passion
    Still lives; your dancing lives as long
        As grace; "extinct" is a misnomer.

4.

Because sly Darwin liked the Fit
    And Mendel, good gray monk, sowed peas,
        Dame Evolution said benignly,
"My child, get bigger," and you did;
    "Look here, those silly toes must cease!"
        And you grew hoofs and frisked equinely.

5.

When you were dodging dinosaurs
    So recklessly, they were gigantic,
        But look how nature turns the tables:
Now they, who scared you with their roars,
    Have changed to lizards, wee and frantic,
        And you're immense and live in stables.

6.

Ballet-star of our mammal race,
Last lingering of earth's first grace,
Dance on in this museum case.

The Sleepdancers

One crunch of fangs is all the thanks I'd get,
Were I to join the waltz behind their bars.
I tried to look away but shan't forget
This circus dance of sixteen mangy bears.

Their jowls, like good sports in a comic paper,
Grin their Indignity. Explore that word.
Your "injured and insulted," here they caper.
I wish I really thought they were absurd.

And do *you* think so, snout-chained soul of man,
You audience whose paws erupt that rumpus?
You middle-aged and grouchy, gypped of fun.
You growlers all, inelegantly pompous.

And tell me, do they sleepdance, just like you?
Nightly do they keep step, the whole sixteen,
When on the roof their plumpness teeters through
The canvas of the carnival-canteen?

Beneath the roof, their chainer is carousing.
If he but guessed what bear-hugs overhead
Flatten the moon they fly to when they're drowsing . . .
Suppose they crash? *Who shrives bears when they're dead?*

Shall cats and curs, that cringed to watch them lope,
Now dice to divvy and lug home their fat?
If I'm around, I'll put a stop to that.
I'll honor gaucheness anywhere I find it

And the deep sadness of a shaggy hope.

The New Cultural Blues *

1. The Culture-Hug Muse

We no longer starve culture; we SWITCH
And hug it to death; the new PITCH
Is to croon antiquarian love-that-librarian CULture-hug blues.
When Status Quo feels safe enough to ITCH
For scripts that let it laugh at its own TWITCH,
What's big bold "beat" bohemia but Babbitt's latest NICHE?
When "liberal" is but a stance and "Tory" but a pout
And "radical" a tease to get still more for selling out,
When suburbs shriek with tongue-in-chic,
When ads for fads ape art-technique,
They all croon the CULture-hug blues.

If she isn't culture-snooty, there's a cooty on your cutie;
It's the duty of a beauty to be arty at a party,
Smarty with CULtural ooze.
For Madison Avenue's guilt at its revenues, what is the medicine? BLUES!
Not your mass-culture booze but our SENsitive muse,
Our anti-vulgarian, NEo-vulgarian, culture-hug blues.
If genius is an infinite capacity for faking PAINS,
Our Weltschmalz tears erase our huckster STAINS.
Art is an exorcism better than bell, book, and COUCH;

* When performed to music at Harvard's Loeb Theater in 1961, the stage
directions were as follows. The first "blues" song is by three Madison Avenue executives in gray flannels; the second by the three Furies, dressed as
progressive club-women, tossing a plastic-bag globe. Only one speaker at a
time, but chorus at refrains. Each capitalizing of a whole syllable is cue
for exaggerated loudness and vowel-lingering; all non-capitalized syllables
of such a line get chanted in unaccented monotone.

We're three blind Sensitive Plants, see how we wince, ouch ouch OUCH.
We've got to play with boors by day in order to stock our LARder;
We put to flight that guilt at night by hugging culture HARder;
A cultural ouch does more than the couch to purge that guilty ARdor.
From cash's clink aghast we shrink, to prove we can afFORD it;
With snoot held high we pass it by, because we've already STORED it;
High sen-ti-ment plus six per cent need never hug the SORdid:—
Except in office HOURS, except in office HOURS.
Culture is like a FOReign rug; we hate its looks but need its hug
To prove we can afFORD it, to prove we can afFORD it.

We're crisp executives at dawn, *poètes maudits* at dusk,
But even a sensitive weed must feed its HUSK;
The culture we hug is a culture for dusk,
An afterthought culture, a rarefied musk,
And not for office HOURS.
That's why, no matter how soulful we wince,
Our culture-hug muse and your mass-culture muse
Are identical sisters under their skins:
Both whore with who can afFORD it.

II. The World-Lobotomy Muse

Now when dacha nouveau-riche and hot-cha profit itch
Merge brands,
When brain-wash sociology and sublim-ad psychology
Join hands,
When Pepsi-Cola toasts unite vulgarians of all LANDS [1]
And "peace" means the homogenizing global churn of kitsch,
You'll be FORCED to croon the global lobal blues.
First they toasted, then they tiffed;
Yet through summit OR through rift
Here's a truth will never shift while any bureaucrat comMANDS:
Human heads will get short shrift from RObot hands.

[1] Dispatch of July 27, 1959: "Today two of the world's leading statesmen and rivals—an American vice-president, a Russian dictator—exchanged Pepsi-Cola toasts in Moscow, at an American kitchen-exhibit dedicated to their common aim of industrial progress."

So strike up all Rotarian plus proletarian
Pan-barbarian BANDS.

Progress is a PLAStic bag;
Come stick in your head and what AILS you will sag,
Gasping the BLUE-in-the-face blues.
When our propaganda spasms turn your isms into wasms,
We'll bag the earth in a PLAStic globe and disconnect your frontal lobe
With our gadget-pop Agitprop air-jet-hop think-no-more blues.

In the oldfashioned day, to make citizens stay reliable pals of big BROther,
There were salt mine and whip, but now we just snip
       the gray stuff that causes the BOther.
That snip is metaphorical, its blade a doctored word;
For the pen of the rhetorical is mightier than the sword;
And the blanker the grin, the blander within,
When a tranquilized planet must spin to the din
Of the world-lobotomy blues.
Let justice wobble sloppily in monolith monopoly;
Forget about Thermopylae; let Hungary bleed properly;
Cringe happily, vox populi, and dream it saves your skin—
       While your global-lobal muse, when she muses on NEWS,
       Keeps keening these meaningless Mother Goose blues:
       "Little boy Geiger, come blow your horn;
       There's beep in the meadow, there's borsht in the corn.
       Rockabye fallout, on top of the show;
       When the wind blows you, the tuna will glow; [2]
       When the nerve BREAKS, Humpty Dumpty will fall;
       Down will come baby, CULture and all."

1959

---

[2] News item: "Japanese fishermen, down-wind of the American atomic test, have been complaining that their tunas shine in the dark."

Aging Refugee from the Old Country

(sentimental folk-jingle of the slum cafés, time uncertain)

1.

Somewhere I'll find you in this too inscrutable town,
Girl whom I love since your bravely patched coat brushed my shoulder.
Though your veil was too thick for your shy foreign face to show bolder,
Yet the refugee newspaper, halfway concealed in your gown,
And the lilt of your heels so hopeless and homeless and proud
Branded you one of us, girl I then lost in the crowd.
Somewhere I'll find you in this too anonymous town.

2.

Somewhere I'll find you in this too alien town,
Girl I still search for, though since then a decade has gone.
Vainly I've sketched them your coat in the pawnshops we clutter,
Hocking some last high-fidelity gadget for butter.
It was done just so little to *them*—was that much to forgive?
It is "tolerant," doubtless, to grudgingly let us few live;
But we refugees tire of hearing what "thanks" we must give.
Will I never yet find you in this sanctimonious town?

3.

Somewhere I'll find you in this too indifferent town,
Girl whom the crowd wrenched my heart from a decade ago.
Pavements I felt once, faces that burnt into dust,
You can restore them, you are what home I still know.
Vainly I've traced you through every remaining café
That still lets our people pass hats for a smoke or a crust.
Vainly I've trudged through each bar where a coke can still sell,
Where our old ones play checkers and savor our half-extinct speech:

"Your move"—but then always: "and where were you when it fell?"
Will I find you mothlike tonight at Old Telescope Beach
(Where our people face over and over again through the spray
The shimmer, the shimmer where once North America lay)?
Is it there I will find you at last in this Japanese town?

I Am an Old Town-Square

Come closer, build on me. . . . My land has wrapped her
History round me in a sevenfold quilt,
Whose layers are towns.
                        A crass and tinny scepter,
Such as the brasher kind of dynasts tilt,

Is all my courtyard holds of my first tribe.
Their names? Their fame? No interesting guilt
Of Overreach coaxed footnotes from a scribe;
Their centuries were rain my gutter swilled.

Such songless trudgers it was joy to jilt.
I became a dirge black crows, black coffins shrilled.
Plague was my second town. Plague snowed those black
Song-notes across my granite music rack.

Next, pilgrims found that coffin-wood and built
A pleasure town of wine and love. (My third.)
A thousand years they belched and strewed their milt.
What did time save of them? One dried up turd.

A trade-town's fourth, with art so polychrome—
Such holiness from huckstering distilled—
That sudden shaggy nomads, wolfskin-frilled,
Would rather starve there than be khans at home.

My fifth town downright pranced with buccaneerings.

Loot gave my cobblestones a jingly lilt.
The night my floor was starry-skied with ear-rings,
Sackfuls of ear-lobes clogged my drains like silt.

My sixth was reared by knights who hanged those raiders.
Its saintly prayer was, "Vengeance to the hilt."
Gouged by Love's camp of gallows and crusaders,
My scars are chinks where armored knees have knelt.

Time passed.
        Those chinks lodged clover.
                        Smoke said, "Wilt."
Desert of smokestacks. But a bee had smelt
A bud, and soon my seventh town consoled
My claws of soot with rings of buzzing gold.

A dream:—From eighth cocoon my airiest city
Spreads glittering wings, true gold now, nothing gilt.
Around me twirls a tinkling live confetti
Of childhoods. Ancient pavements bask fulfilled;

And rustling down each twilight, slim on porches,
Tiptoe on spires like willowy stilt on stilt,
Shimmers of girlhood—aspen glances—pelt
My yard with fireflies from soft-browed torches.

A dream . . . it never came. Death came. Death spilt.
Was this my eighth cocoon? Then why unbuilt
My wings? Come look, how rich I am with stone!
Why am I left to . . . radiate alone?

Homecoming

(a charade on "civilized" hedonism and its eventual purgatory through moral isolation)

My seven sons came back from Indonesia.
Each had ruled an atoll twenty years alone.
Twenty years of loneliness, twenty years of craziness,
Of hell's and Eden's silence on an exiled coral throne.
My six grunting sons had forgotten what a language is;
My seventh was a warlock, chanting every language known.

My seven sunburnt sons arrived at the airport.
The airport had a banner up. Its words were "WELCOME HOME."
The mayor made a speech, and the virgins rainbowed over them
The many-tongued hooray of confetti's polychrome.
But, though seven new Rolls-Royces sped them richly to my parlor,
They only filed their long sharp teeth; the warlock's were afoam.

The day before my seven sons returned from atoll-loneliness,
The butler starched his livery to welcome them in style;
"*Thé dansant* for the young masters?" gushed the housemaid,
          strewing doilies;
I bought my sons a set of Proust to titillate their guile.
My seven Dresden China cups were waiting, hot with tea;
And all was ready as my sons tramped in. They didn't smile.

"You homesick boys from far-off Indonesia,
Relax and romp," I said, "and know you're loved.
It's true that twenty years alone with coral
Is not God's hand at its most velvet-gloved.
But let's test your sense of humor; don't be morbid;
I'll get tantrums if my welcome is rebuffed."

Did they listen? No, they only watched the seventh . . .
Till he made a kind of signal. Then they roared and went amok.
Two swung from chandeliers and pounced on the butler.
Two held the maid down and clawed off her smock.
Two ate the Proust set. "Be careful, kids," I wheedled;
"Romp all you like but spare my teacups any shock.

"I can buy you chubby housemaids by the dozen.
You can eat a butler, even eat a book.
But whoever chips—no matter who—my china,
He'll get magicked back to nature's loneliest nook."
"No matter who?" the warlock asked—and tripped me
Right across my magic teacups. I awoke

On this hellish, Eden-beautied reef of coral
In a perfect climate full of perfect food,
Where my sense of humor's tested by the silence
And I've nothing else to do but fish and brood.
"Sons, come back and get me out of Indonesia!"
But, of course, they couldn't hear me. No one could.

The Lyricism of the Weak

I sit here with the wind is in my hair;
I huddle like the sun is in my eyes;
I am (I wished you'd contact me) alone.

A fat lot you'd wear crape if I was dead.
It figures, who I heard there when I phoned you;
It figures, when I came there, who has went.

Dogs laugh at me, folks bark at me since then;
"She is," they say, "no better than she ought to";
I love you irregardless how they talk.

You should of done it (which it is no crime)
With me you should of done it, what they say.
I sit here with the wind is in my hair.

1965

Dance of the Haemophiliacs:

A Ballet for Nietzsche

"HAEMOPHILIA: tendency to prolonged bleeding, even from trifling wound; caused by gene transmitted only by female (e.g., Queen Victoria) but afflicting only her male descendents (e.g., in Span. or Rus. royalty); once called 'the disease of kings.' "

Part I: Charades

"The very laws of the planet are a lie and the vaudeville of devils."
—KIRILLOV

Circling a flag (whose code eludes its readers)
In an opaque meander of a wood,
The secret congregation of the bleeders
Deliberates on how to hoard its blood.

There's not a jack-knife in the whole pavilion;
No scissors ever thin a forehead's thatch;
No point or bump or edge to ooze vermillion.
"What most we trust may mask the fatal scratch."

It's rubbery, their world; it's all amok;
Elations bounce it, panic snaps it back.
"Our needle test for a suspected spy:
Unless he bleeds to death, he's guilty and must die."

Their forest hide-away becomes a stealthy

Armageddon: bleeders versus clotters.
Their cornucopia of torrent shatters
Against the treacle of the healthy.

A *thé dansant* for ghosts of martyred leaders.
Two pouting chins flap by, like bats of witch:
Infante's *pas de deux* with czarevitch.
Dawn crows. And God gets begged, "Protect all bleeders.

"All earth is Dracula to us and wheedles
Our fatal tide, but where You're overhead
We know we're safe." A sudden wind. The needles
From evergreens rain on the ever red.

"Betrayed again." They blubber for new saviors,—
A meat-heap twitched by maggot-nips of faith.
Above, the cosmic disinfector savors
The vintage incense of a stagey death.

They caper, then, like heels an adder triggers;
They try to shake their fists, but pudgily,—
Contorted less by bone's corporeal rigors
Than by mind's rage at undeserved decree.

That gene, that egg of anger, who plants it in a bleeder?
In howl and hunger shriller, what non-man monster Other?
"In claw and skull-fur longer; red-lipt like unclean feeder;
Of nest, of trap a builder; 'hi,' says the prey, 'hi mother'."

The Other has enforcements, frisking cutely
As home and culture, decency—and duty.
"Concretely: sagging breasts and drive-in tombs,
Gold toilet seats—and devil mobs with bombs."

The bleeders' flag is coded: "two visions of our lady."
On one side Queen Victoria squats benign,
Grandma of death-pale kinglets. The other side is bloody:
A female spider, dirty and divine.

Part II: Clown Priests

"Pro me autem nihil gloriabor nisi in infirmitatibus meis."
—II Cor. 11:30

Even in May, their clock is autumn.
Even at dawn, their face is west.
Even at birth, their breast was orphan.
Yet moonlight tans them, shade can warm, in such a breast.

For castaways, no lamp except obsession.
When steered by, doubted, steered by through the brine,
At last the tight beam widens, lights an ocean.
With truth? With myth?—With pain, not anodyne.

Their pain might tune all pain,
                              with bellows' patience
Might fan to art the arson of the injured.
But no: the clown priests of exsanguinations
Hug outward power closer now than inward.

Are research labs inventing quicker styptic?
Do millions shave by plugging in a cord?
Are hat pins out of fashion? Smiling cryptic,
A secret bleeder hugs his power hoard.

Or civic jargons: storming prison,
They jail the jailers, make more locks.
"We ban the blood-red dagger." . . . Poison
Caressingly turns blue whoever mocks.

Or so they daydream, till the hubris pops.
Inebriates of overcompensation,
They sip the pride of granite domination,
These khans more fragile than their porcelain cups.

No flavor to the sip. For, watching tacit,
The one small spidery gene sucks dry their powers.
Confront, confront? "Without a prop, can't face it.
Halo or scourge, at least uniquely ours."

136

And so (romantics, choosing incompleteness)
Each pirouettes his separate tragic stance.
But what avails a bleeding-throated sweetness?
The dancers know they chose the lesser dance.

One out of step then (clouds of gnats afflict him)
Bleeds free, an outcast even from the out:
      "Why cult your wound? All blood, theirs too, is victim—
      Is ink, is ode. Man's dare beyond man's doubt.

      "A thing is falling,
                        lights all windowpanes;
      A sky more likely than a firecracker.
      Not faucets quench a falling God but veins.
      Though hardly yours, chic bleeders
                        of red lacquer."

But pirouetting through the pines and cedars
Whose evergreen, they hope, protects their blood,
The secret congregation of the bleeders
Deliberates on how to stanch its flood.

1966

9: Two Scenes from a Play*

* These are scenes four and seven from the verse-play *The Tree Witch* (Charles Scribner's Sons, New York: 1961, out of print). All literary and stage rights belong to the author; no scripts or book copies are available except through the author; no performance without his permission. West German stage and book rights have been bought by the Cologne publishers Kiepenheuer & Witsch, who are bringing out a German translation by Peter Borchardt, director of the Cologne State Theater. The play has been performed by Harvard's Loeb theater, the Cape Ann Players (Rockport, Mass.), the Kanawha Players (State Theater of Charleston, West Virginia), and other experimental groups in America and Europe, including Poland.

Over a dozen lyrics in other chapters of the present volume are also excerpted from *The Tree Witch*, including "The Aphrodite Trilogy," "In the Month of March," and "The Reaching Out of Warmth."

Dramatis Personae of *The Tree Witch*

SHE: The Hellenic dryad, captured (and jailed in a garage) when WE chop down her tree to make way for an eight-lane highway.

WE: The enlightened and emancipated technologizing moderns.

THEY: Our three guardians, the hygiene-spraying and jargon-spraying aunts, who in a later scene turn out to be the vengeful Eumenides (hell hath no woman like a Fury scorned) struggling with Aphrodite's emissary, the dryad, for the soul of WE.

Scene 4, Songs As Actions: The Autumn Maneuver *

[WE *and* SHE *in yard outside garage, we separated from her by side-curtain, around which we eavesdrop; she facing tree with dark late-summer foliage.*]

SHE: Outside my window is a wall of green;
I see no higher than a tree is tall;
I see no further than a leaf allows;
Where is October and the harvest-glean?
I hear no thud of plum beyond the wall;
Between the grape and me, a wall of green;
How long since last I was a god and rose
As cadence of the wine-press festival?
    [*twining with tree*]
    I knew, from inside once, this very green;
    It was my skin; and tingling I recall
    How just this tint, when just so rich it flows,
    Would drain my roots to feed my tallest boughs.

* Highway billboard: "MANEUVER 4, THE DEFEAT OF LEAVES."

141

Seeing now such fullness, my whole body knows
So deep in summer is not far from fall.

[*Enter aunts.*]

THEY [*to us*]:
Three lost maneuvers: humbling, bribing, flying.
Autumn—the fourth—will make her own hopes fail.
We planted her old tree-home, before fall,
Outside her window so she'll watch it failing.
Make her howl dirges on the death befalling
What grows. Triumphant metals feel no fall.

[*Aunts rip off side-curtain that separated her from us, redrape it so as to hide tree from audience, and leave stage. At our fourth line below, we restore tree to view; tree has meanwhile been changed from late-summer to autumn, with a single large red leaf. During first two lines, we point at painted backdrop of modern apartments.*]

WE [*to her*]:
In the conditioned kits we rarely leave,
Our in-grown Spring need brave no season's falling.
Yet out we've stept to see your old tree failing,
And so to strip you of your old belief,—
While clinics tape-record, without your leave,
Melodies maundered for your own relief:
    Three voices of autumn (from your tree-harp falling
    As crisscross as the drift of falling leaf).

SHE: The first two are the autumn dialogue
Of Ouranos and Gaia, sky and earth,
The father and the mother you forgot.
First, Father Ouranos, as if serenading:—

[*First and second autumn songs—staged as dialogue—are accompanied by* tableau vivant *of sky serenading and then embracing earth; sky as male actor, reaching down from suspended cotton cloud; earth as actress in wheat-costume, reaching up from autumnal orchard.*]

If through a wind I ripple every tide
With such a wave as rattles every quay,
It is to haunt the true lost flesh they hide;
All seas, all soils but sheathe my bride from me.

Her skirt of colored seasons crowns her thighs
And circles round the lunar tune she sways.
—O loose your sweet green locks with drowsy grace
And slowly brush their warmth across my eyes.

Twisting your shoulder-blades beneath the plow
That fondles you when apple twigs are bent,
Deep in your hills you would not huddle so
If you believed how sad I am you went.

Then let no princeling of the apricots
Excite you with the ripeness of the year.
His nectared cheeks must burst; your courtier rots;
My snows are on his trail, will soon be here.

And yet am sun. I nibble listlessly
A ghat of all the wives of all my whims.
Autumnal tawny harems burn for me.
Such games will not distract me from your limbs.

Call to me dawdlingly when summer falters.
Attract me bitterly through molten grain.
I am your sky; look up; my clouds are altars
To worship you with desecrating rain.

SHE: Now earth's reply, invoking the autumn instant:—

Then touch the park; the leaves are stained to lure you.
The leaves are spread on winds they fan befòre you.
They drained the summer, and their veins prefèr you,
Dark with the season they are droning for.

Then bring the heavy dying they prefer.
Each painful fruit is hanging heavier.

Why pause when loveliness grows lonelier
And love is just as melting as it looks?
There's but one touch that all the ripeness lacks:
You are the instant; you are waited for.

Then never wait when flutes of foliage bear you
Home on the homeward tune they always bore.
Fear not at all the twigs of flame they bear.
These never meant to be a barrier.
The lovely are as lonely as their gleam,
The lonely just as loving as they seem,
The fruits as melting as they always were:
There is a fondling they are furtive for.

Then touch my park. The leaves have spread befòre you
The green they drained, the darkness they prefer.
Come to the leaves, reach out and touch them all.
Bring to the smoldering year, that hovers fòr you,
The hovering instant love is dawdling for:

There's not one leaf that does not long to fall.

● ● ●

WE: Your swarthy Gaia, all these Levantines,
Keep sidling up to hawk Olympic tours
While we watch our purse.
                         You owe us one more autumn.
But bring myth up-to-date first. For example,
Just what was Aphrodite up to after
The clock struck One A.D.? Fill in such blanks.
Come edify us with some wholesome ballad.

SHE: A short-line ballad makes me scan my sister
By her more parvenu short Roman name.
Venus Venus Sister Venus.

WE: Sister? Then Ouranos strews seed like autumn!
As heard on TV's "Myth Made Easy" hour,

144

His famous wound strewed blood as much as foam.
We know whom foam bred on the sea. But blood?

SHE: Blood bred the tree nymphs on the land. Love's sisters.
(And bred the Furies, fortunately gone.)
My father dies in every leaf that bleeds,
And every leaf will find my mother's lap.

WE: Sing Venus, but make her inspirational:
Prize-pupil's recitation-piece in pigtails
Of fallen female salvaged by repentance.

[*Meanwhile dryad slips on costume of a modern "Magdalen"; perhaps flaunted furs, long and tight black evening dress. Swinging long cigarette holder, she strides up and down in rhythm with her "BALLAD OF MAGGIE JONES":–*]

SHE:
Is it HER voice, repenting repentance
We hear when a mattress groans?
What goddess haunts the downstairs couch
Whenever Smith dates Jones?

Let other birds chirp for your prizes
On wrists too comfy to leave.
I sing for the sons who'll defy you
And the daughters of Venus, not Eve.

Solve all except me with pure logic;
Computers are rusty junk
When a girl is a jigsaw-puzzle
And a boy is the solving chunk.

Cold nights and callous mornings;
Dirt clings to all we own.
Then cling to each other, soiled children;
Cry we must, but at least not alone.

WE: Not what we ordered. Fool. Misunderstood.
Croon how love's goddess, renamed Magdalena,
Now wears low heels and brings sick soldiers water.

SHE: What's Venus up to anyhow
        Now that her doves are crows?
        She plays THE BALLAD OF MAGGIE JONES
        And here is how it goes . . .

        After I give them lust or birth,
        They all crawl out and cry.
        I tuck them back, they still won't stay
        In any womb but sky.

        My love needs dollars, his needs souls,
        Mine is the cheaper fee.
        My quicksand hugs for half a night,
        His for eternity.

        I've nothing at all to heal the sick
        Except myself to share,
        My few warm inches of cosiness
        Against his eons of air.

        So what could I do but join his troupe?
        My others took and paid.
        My others took and went. He gave,
        Seduced my soul, and stayed.

        What else could I do but bathe his feet?
        His magic seemed stronger than mine—
        Till Smith's boy, Judas, rang my bell,
        More drunk with the bread than the wine.

        Young Judas kissed my breasts and said,
        "Eternity's too old.
        I hate the skies I cannot touch.
        I hate his love; it's cold."

WE: Too long for a ballad. Only three more stanzas allowed.

SHE: That Judas wisdom freed me.
        Glum centuries ensued:
        The lioness thrown to the Christians,
        Venus crucified.

146

Then why do I bring them water
And nurse each time their ache?
Because my only creed is
Warmth for its own crude sake.

I don't much like humanity.
My love is lilt, not vow.
I warm, each time, not mankind but
One near one, here and now.

[*Speaking above last stanza at exit-door,* SHE *leaves stage with air of leaving for a rendez-vous.*]

WE: That was all a distraction to make us forget her promise
Of three autumn voices; we've counted only two, and
She's playing for time because the third voice, being
Dirge of the seasons, is the forlornest.
The seasons: door-guards of Olympos once,
Demoted now to functionless adornments
In the conditioned Spring we rarely leave,—
Their shattered circle
[*shrugging at re-entering dryad*]
               hers.

SHE: [*back in Greek tunic*]:
Voice of the seasons, the obsessed returners,
Voice of the seasons (to leaves, in leaf-drift rhythms):—*

    Like actors in a death-scene played with poise
    Lest rant make critics smile or scare small boys,
    You fall. No blood, no blenching.
    Only the dry red wrenching.

    Leaves on panes,

---

* Her third autumn voice gets acted as alternation of long and short cadences, moodily drifting, addressed to red leaf on tree between backdrops of tractor and church-centered galaxy. Actor intonation and off-stage music are low and slow when accompanying short, heavy-voweled lines like "Leaves on loam"; high and spry when accompanying long, quick-voweled lines like "Dead children knocking to be let back in."

Wistful for the green so briefly borrowed.
Then the rain's
Fiddling on the twigs so newly sorrowed.

Leaves on loam,
Dead children knocking to be let back in.
Each has been
Tree-top-dizzy while so high from home.

Sweet and swift,
Your first careen on air; then crushed to be
Waif of drift
Between the tractor and the galaxy.

Yet joy is what they crush you to,
The work machine and the world machine.
Kiss of the wine-press festival, renew
Red lips of autumn with the pledge of green.

They'll have their autumn too,
Machine and machine.
Next year not they re-green,
Outfading you.

Flawless their clockwork-flash;
Leaf drags with loam;
Falling from speed to ash,
Not they fall home.

Leaves in space:
Vintage whose radiance outshines a ray's.
Leaf on steel:
Rainbow whose year outspins a wheel.

Spin death and beauty (year now sere, now heady),
Opposites—feuding, fornicating—in
Green already
Reddening.

Not godless joy or joyless God,
Machined as "good for" or as "good,"

But doom made sweet in art and
Bloom out of bloom-dust gardened.

Fuse death and beauty (leaf now red, now green),
Infinites in a wisp of sheen;
Fuse forth the specter no mirrors mirror,
That last of the temples, that innermost terror,

Between the tractor and the galaxy
That marble hammered from mortality:
The clay which is the self-surpass of clod,
The gods who are dishevelment of God.

Then warmth is what the clockworks crush you to,
The wheels and rays;
O fullness of the festive wine-press, strew
A throb of colors through the ice of space.

Then flutter the green joy of your red going;
A color was a thirst when you were growing;
A color is a promise today when you fall.
Triumphant falling leaf, you are the strongest thing of all.

Scene 7, Panic in Arcady

[*Left backdrop: tidy business office. Right: thicket labeled "AR-
CADY."* we *enter out of breath and plead with dryad.*]

we: We're on the lam from aunts
                              and from six lost maneuvers.
Inveigle from your slummy halfgod contacts
A hide-out for us in the land of Id.
What's going on beyond the schoolhouse hedges?
Fix us with some delirious new spasm
Out there among those reeds and all those pipings.
Here
[*gesturing at business office*]
     every racy action comes vicarious;

High jinks are as atrophied as the word "thus";
Everything's organized, and "thus" a bore.

SHE: Too late. You're filed in your own filing-system
With frayed manila-folders for your souls—
Once labeled "GOD'S OWN IMAGE: USE WITH CARE"
But now reclassified as "OBSOLETE."

WE: Serve us Arcadia, bodily and direct.
Brew us a Trip, witch, to outjump our skins,
To live on fresher levels even if brute ones,
As psychodelic panic did where Pan was.

SHE: Passionate in Arcady? For once unvicarious?
Why, of course. I, illusionist, herb-brewer,
Reach you this jug of ironies. A gulp is your springboard.

[WE *drink from her jug and bound from business backdrop to
Arcady backdrop. During our long hallucinated speech that follows,
nothing we describe—orgy, trampling, or Pan—is really there, except
for a single ordinary goat.*]

WE [*to each other*]:
We've jumped to Arcady like champagned corks. Action
Thrums us like tics. We feel unleashed. We feel
Nature and naked freedom everywhere.
[*staggering violently, dazedly*]
Is it lava or waterfalls? . . . in either case
Shagginess comes at us. All over us. O and now
The goats themselves, cartoons of our own dawn.
But toothier. Bucking. The air steamy with wishes.
Look!—hooves are trampling the nipples of gross breasts;
The stare of noon winks its indulgence; we'll join them,
Rearing our shin bones, gymnasts of orgy,
Slobbering with surrealist derring-do.
　　　　　　[*we rough-house with office furniture:*]
　　　　　　Bellowing and walloping up and down verandas,
　　　　　　Past widened eyes of courtiers and aghast cats,
　　　　　　We throw chairs at each other; the air is splintry with wood;—

[*seeing one small crow:*]
     Storms of black snowflakes caw into our ears.
[*Eerie pipings off-stage.*]
From goats that gods in heat have rubbed against,
From noon-mad thickets horned with shaggy hints,
An ancientness of winds in reed-pipes pities us:—

UNSEEN PAN VOICE [*from direction of goat and thicket*]:
Gardening their wishes, terrace over terrace,
My vineyard children knew: what counts is levels.
Your lusts are outburst, and you call them nature;
But on what level and with what a snigger!
Poison for you: the wines without the wine-god,
Our naked freedom without our measured dance.
Better than you: even my desert Foeman
And all His disproportion of sky to loam.
Better that drouth than hydroponic passions.
Sweeter that death than automats of life.

[WE *bound back to right stage, in "panic."*]

WE: Goodbye to Arcady; Pan scared us so we
Jumped all the way home,
                     to this day reeking of goat.
. . . Trance. Jug. What did you do to us, witch?

SHE: [*matter-of-fact voice*]:
The brew was water. The rest you supplied yourselves.

10: Walks

"The race is almost meaningful."
—*page 168*

A Walk on Snow

Pine-trail; and all the hours are white, are long.
But after miles—a clearing: snow and roundness.
Such circle seemed a rite, an atavism,
A ripple of the deep-plunged stone of myth.
I crossed that ring to loiter, not to conjure.
Stood in the centre as in melodrama.
Wondered: if the centre were a gate?
A gate from earth to non-earth? Gate where fingers,
Where rays perhaps, are fumbling signals through?
         Or are stars cold for all their brightness,
Deaf to our urgencies as snowflakes are?
Then magic blazed: a star spoke through the gate:
"I am not cold; I am all warm inside."

At once new longing charged and shook the air
Like spreading tremors of a storm's spilt moan.
Star-tunes lured old tellurian lonelinesses.
Like chord-joined notes of one sky-spanning octave,
Orbs blent in universal tremolo.
         "Star, star, reachable star,
Truly," I called, "you are all warm inside."
Shy through the gate came answer, frail in space:
"Good luck, brother. It's not so far across."

Being absurd as well as beautiful,
Magic—like art—is hoax redeemed by awe.
(Not priest but clown, the shuddering sorcerer
Is more astounded than his rapt applauders:
"Then all the props and Easters of my stage
Came true? But I was joking all the time.")

Art, being bartender, is never drunk;
And magic that believes itself, must die.
My star was rocket of my unbelief,
Launched heavenward as all doubt's longings are;
  It burst when, drunk with self-belief,
I tried to be its priest and shouted upward:
"Answers at last! If you'll but hint the answers
For which earth aches, that famous whence and whither;
Assuage our howling Why with final fact."

At once the gate slammed shut, the circle snapped,
The sky was usual and broad and silent.
A snowflake of impenetrable cold
Fell out of sight incalculably far.
Ring all you like, the lines are disconnected.
Knock all you like, no one is ever home.
(Unfrocked magicians freeze the whole night long;
Holy iambic cannot thaw the snow
They walk on when obsessive crystals bloom.)
Shivering I stood there, straining for some frail
Or thunderous message that the heights glow down.
  I waited long; the answer was
The only one earth ever got from sky.

1933

A Walk on Moss

I

Two lovers walking in a lovers' garden,
Dreaming old books with heavy-lidded pages
About two lovers walking in a garden.
They walk as dawdlingly as bark uncurls,

More inwardly than deep green lavishes;
They walk as timelessly as moss spells out
To every step the Braille of "dream forever,"
Where "forever" means an hour's walk on moss.
His eyes that drowse too open, dream illusions:
That worlds—what kind?—exist outside the garden.
Then just in time both dim their eyes—to wake;
And then she sees no grief on earth beyond
The hint of pebbles in a sandal or
A starling lost in rhododendron bushes.

II

Two lovers, speaking in a garden, spangling
Confetti of tropes. In fun articulating
Extravagant picnics of sound. Let her say: "I am
A mere coiffure of baubles who thank the sun,
'It is your noon that loans us stellar ways.'"

"If head-dress," let him answer, "then Milky Way.
A pompadour of terraced fireflies.
An intricacy of comets at toss of the head,
A disciplined waterfall of well-tuned skies."

"Then you, disheveler of cosmic primness,
It is who orchestrates that luminary
Lustre as startlingly as combs in winter."
And he: "Swim, tortoise-shell, on such sweet tides!"

So let them speak—like Byzantines of love—
A minute in fun, their courtship having been
In truth least courtierlike of pastorals,
Needing each other as simply as fetching water
From stillness of wells. Two lovers, two true loves:
As inarticulate as bread is shared.

III

A garden of togethers, waifs of groves,
Two twigs slender as rain, leaning

157

As tenderly as eyelids almost-meet.
Or else an "ah" and "oh," a pair of breaths
So in, so through, so hoveringly past
Corporeal gates as if two sighs were drifting
Through sultry, gnat-stirred southlands, fluttered at
By dusks of moth-eyed, mild astonishments.
Yet lovers both: branded to the bone with knowledge,
Stifled to the lungs with incense of fulfillment,
Stained with each other's scents like painter's palettes.
Palettes whose perfect white is white and isn't,
Being blended from all colors ever tried.
Dark and pure their thicket of entangling;
Dark and heavy its cloying; darkly white
The gentleness—heavy, heavy—of the gorged lovers.

IV

From time to time they watch a goldfish circling.
Beside white groves. The shade of saplings covers
The pond as chastely as a shadow longs.
White shadow, ceremoniously emblemed
With slow wet rings that fade as sad as gold does.
What have they to do—touching, as they walk,
Only each other's knowing fingertips—
What have they to do, satiated and kind,
Two lovers in a garden-walk, what else
But watch a rainbow of fins paddle like petals
Across a mirrored indolence of birches?
More real than they themselves are, for an hour
Is not the only solid stuff in dreamland
The slow wet gold reflected from the circlings
Of fish on the reflected white of bark?
Here limbs are air, and contours cannot press.
And only surfaces are deep.
And nothing true except reflectedness.

V

Here and now, nothing is willed, and nothing touches;

Not even the slowed up air—westering breezelessly—
Ripples the gauze of her shoulders. For an hour,
Luxuriance has grown past wantonness; has grown
Back down into a bud, as darkly pure
As satin, as unfolded as cocoons. . . .
And so two lovers walking in a garden
Became one moon. Pure white, drained beyond fire,
One moon in empty skies,
Rich beyond clouds and to itself enough.

1953

Five Roman Cadences

(composed during 1944–1956)

1. Fontana Delle Naiadi
(fountain rhythms)

1.

Forgetfully
My fountains play
Glass symphonies
To arm my peace.
Such tides efface
Such tunes replace
An older peace,
My other days,
Of you the day.
     Rebelliously
     Resounding out
     Of mountains came
     Marvel: a shout:
     "I am the same."

Who is that singing
Through my song?
       Reluctantly
       Returns at last
       Memory,
       Monody.
       Wild with a lilt
       Fountains lack
       (They never burn),
       Love turns back,
       You return:
       "I waited long;
       I never changed."

3.

Implacably
Your unestranged
Unrest came:
A shout: "The same!"
Out of the mountains
Echoing.
       How fragilely
       Now suddenly
       These arms of glass
       Grope, grope and miss,
       Rippling with doubt.
       Splashed by a shout,
       These futile fountains
       Cannot sing.

II. Castel Sant'Angelo

(castle and angel rhythms)

1. (castle rhythms)

Slow
Stone-walled

Immense
Gate,
Dense
As our own old
Sorrow.
>You! angel up there!,
>Can you conquer
>Sheer weight?
Only love's
Feather
Is heavier.

2. (angel rhythms)

Quick
Lightness
Of twig's fall.
Wind's tress
On western wall.
Flick
Of sun's mote.
Grace-note
Music
(Hear the bell
Spill).
>*Only love's*
>*Cruel*
>*Will*
>*Is lighter still.*

III. Borghese Gardens, Viale Dell'Aranciera

(restless pacing rhythms)

1.

In the garden
Where smooth pebbles are
And palm trees next to pine trees

And the many benches there,
A lawn is shining;
It is hedged in by a square.

2.

In the garden
Where the cherub-statues are
And the lake is often looked at
But never with a stare,
The heads of children growing
Out of the shining lawn
Were afraid of the cities;
They were glad the cities were far.

3.

But somewhere is much walking
On desolate dawns;
Somewhere are beaches,
Far from all lawns,
And the lovers the lovers
The lovers walk up and down.

4.

"The world has a thousand cities;
Beware.
The world has a thousand cities,"
Warned a marble garden-child.
"And pains that nobody pities
And lonely sorcerers are there,
And birds have human voices,
And lovers are sick with love,
And the seagulls the seagulls
The seagulls are bitter and wild."

5.

In the garden
Where breezes and benches are kind,

Where grave-eyed heads are growing
But never threateningly,
The mildest head asked sadly,
"For the sake of her eyes and her hair,
To where cities and beaches are,
Why are you going?"
The garden shivered suddenly in all its roots.

6.

"New eyes new hair
Have changed you so,
Now you must go.
Now you must be
Where waters are,"
Said the gentlest statue there.
Now I must sometimes walk
Where they, they . . . the gulls . . . talk.

IV. Lago Di Esculapio
(rhythms of obsession)

Kind as noon, calm of unfalling petals,
Motionless and recurring creek,
Mild park ambushing the ambler,
Warning the lover: "Trespassing Required."

The birds are so light when they land,
Land and hop a little,
So light on the blade of the pond-grass
That it sinks not at all, wings never touch water.

And the blade, the untroubled,
Never even trembling. The pond untingling. The park
Rippled only by the lover, by the rambler saying:

"Always the same." How many times, sometimes with joy,
Has he not said it, and sometimes—"Always the same"—
Desperately? "Always only that face."

v. Frutta Di Stagione

(rhythms of completion)

1.

"Fruit of the season" so your menu ends.
"Frutta di stagione," phrase to speak aloud
As slow as branches bend with what they grow.
Then spread the menu out you never wrote;
What gentleness, to flower as slow as seasons,
You of a season, Valerie Sophia.

2.

What sadness also: outlawed from outstaying,
Trust least the closest linkages with boughs.
Juices of the season, of one season only,
Yet altogether that; how goldenly—
These overfilled crescendos of a brim—
They toast the sun round every spoke it slants.
Potion of love . . . and sleep, a wheeling goblet,
A rim of sun around a hub of fruit.
Then, fearless, kiss that brim when offered to you;
Savor it—gulp—twist dripping, drenched at last with
The molten lime-tang of finality.

3.

How many days how far from here there dangled,
Bountiful spendthrifts of themselves, these orbs,
To pile a plate for Valerie Sophia.
Plumaged with twilight, figs swayed ever looser,—
Blue parrots fanned by ever huger ferns.
And nameless southern plants of fiercer nectars
Once basked as secret as suspicions, brewing
Liqueurs like scorpions brooding in the sun;
Not even they outguile their season's halt.
Beside them foam compressions—apricots,
Once free and airy as the genie was
Before his bottling time, now wedged in peel,

Both cheeks hilarious with flush of doom.
An introspectiveness of olives, depth
In smallness, ebbs each bursting rind back; noons
Nudge all rings coreward. But the blackest glow is
The each day wilder density of dates,
As if all history were pressing inward
All sugar globed into a single ache.

4.

"Last year when I loved Atthis," mourns an echo,
Revolving with an old Ionian year.
Last year when I loved . . . Colors seep away
As melting as the plum-tree's fullest moon.
Receding towards the same invading velvet
That clouds our eyelids two by two by two,
O for the thousand eyes of bees, when death comes,
To savor thousandfold that deepening veil.

5.

Yet simple images compel the more.
"Frutta di stagione," phrase whose slow pride mirrors
Resilient stems when fruits bob shiningly.
And each husk, destined to its own true waning,
Pales vulnerably perfect, Valerie.
Believe the menu, fruits were always so.
Say: "Of the season,"
                            voice as kind as rain;
Believe no branches,
                            eyes as sad as spray.
When destined, tears are seasonable wines.
And each one gentle, Valerie Sophia.

Five Walks on the Edge

(Cape Ann, Massachusetts: Composed 1963–67)

i. Stairs to the Sea

ii. The Entropy Song

iii. A Wreath for a Plunge

iv. More Than Wings Can Bear

v. Counter-Walk, Reversals

i. Stairs to the Sea

1.

(Crisp on the water. Dawn.)
There is one healer and one healer only.
She is not the rose.
There is one solver. He is not the dove.
When love or savior strums us,
Sea is the pulse to drown the sicker pulse.
(Rich on the water. Noon.)

2.

Stoats of the world, winners, chewers: comic,
Choking to death on feathers.
Poor carnivores! It's doves undo us; saviors
Are loose, run for your lives.
There is one healing. It is not on land.
(Shy on the water. Dusk.)

3.

Being a shellfish, not afraid of thorns—
Thorns are afraid of me—

I yet was wounded; thorns may yet conceal
    The hidden, the hurter, the rose.
Come salt, sweet salt, and soothe a petal's bite.
    (Good on the water. Night.)

II. The Entropy Song

1.

The day is opening like a fan.
The gold is dimming anyhow.
At first the gold looks infinite.
The cold erodes it anyhow.
Above our cliff, below our cliff
Two mirrors bounce back blue for blue.
The dialogue looks infinite
Till water drinks the other blue.
    The waves that get, the shores that give
    Don't really seesaw endlessly.
    Yet evenings loiter wistfully:—
    World, world, what wreath from soil so thin?
    The roots replenish till the time
    They don't replenish. Many times
    The warmth is gaining. All the time
    The loss is gaining anyhow.

2.

Have you heard it, have you heard—
"Just a little, just a little"—
Have you heard the tinkling sound?
Cascading down from fall to fall,
The freak is sun. The norm is waste.
We pay to see. The price is night.
Renewed in vain, renewed in vain,
The tinkling sound of light's cascade:
    "Just a little, just a little,"
    Tinkling down from leaf to leaf,

In vain but paid for anyhow.
Yet sun can loiter wistfully:—
Thinning down from worlds to world.
It isn't much we hanker after,
Just a little, just a little
Resonance in so much waste.

3.

The day skims many little days
Like porpoises from wave to wave.
Again the peacock spreads its tail
Across the night. Till night spreads too.
One Light resounding—have you heard?—
Relieves all weight, renews all clocks.
Till running down outweighs them all.
Yet evenings loiter wistfully:—
 World, world, what tune for so much loss?
 What makes your thin-soiled marshland skim
 A hopeless rose from June to June?
 What keeps feet running to your edge?
 The race is almost meaningful.
 The edge is ebbing anyhow.
 Again, again the peacock tail.
 The stars are cooling anyhow.

III. A Wreath for a Plunge

1.

White forehead on green soarings on black dyings,
Every wave is the youngest wave.
A high, a wreath-demanding forehead,
Balanced between surge and tumble,
Every wave is the youngest wave.
Not green for long, the oldest riddle-solver,
Again, again and always for the first time
A white black grave, the only sure solution,

Every wave is the youngest wave.
Come quick across the wrinkles of the marshland,
You others whom no universal star led;
Come ankle-deep—a prince is born—and garland
The perfect whiteness of his newborn forehead,
Every wave being the youngest wave.

2.

"Welcome your prince"—each wave a new imposter,
Forever newly landing with pomp of foam.
"Call me your king"—no end to Bonnie Charlies,
Retreat and Restoration, ebb and tide.
"Am back, my land, to solve your maze the old way"—
Returning exile who never went away.
Or call it cascade of tsars, each False Dimitri
Returning falser and more noble-browed.
"Weave me a welcome of marsh-vine and berries of marshes,
Roots from thin soil, and feathers to add their fern
To the sparse wreath, and grass blown low on marshes."
So wave after wave, each crest a promise
Steadfast as spray.
     Prepare what's left of garlands?
We, fading, hail the even faster fader;
Yes, crown with old pale blossoms of the marshes
The brief pale forehead of the youngest wave.

3.

—His empty forehead. Blank-eyed wave, where are
The shared palaver, the taming, all that junked
Reasonableness to steer by? "Children," say
Only the very old, "I can still remember"
(Birds don't need to remember, their berries are always berries)
"Shared truth."

4.

(Marsh berries

Don't need to be shared. Seagulls

Don't steer by truth.) Waves brought you merely waves.
Waves are a small perfection, no warm answer.
Walk out and pay for what's not floating in:
The Restoration. But this time facing inward,
This time a full, imperfect forehead, earning
A sparse wreath for a risked plunge:
Man's own restoration of man. (Marsh roses
Are beautiful, very pale, beautiful, scentless, beautiful.)
Wade without foresight or don't wade at all.
Plunge without seeing or you'll never find.
There's only insight. (Gulls read maps, their eyes
Look outward; berries, even winds are solid.
Roses are cold. Even warm roses are cold.)
There's only insight, paid for: not a flashlight,
But night probing night. Walk out alone.

5.

One-way footprints. Crossing the edge
Where orphaned sand is eyed by unthroned waves.
What makes him shamble in his probes of blackness?
If crazed, by what? Is he drunk on abstract echoes
Of angel wing-beats, has an angel scared him
Into his wits? And out of lighted sense?
The lights are fading anyhow; the plunges
Are restorations—why should thirst need angels?
It was the thirst itself led to this edge
Of land and breakers, where two frauds confront:
The pseudo-solid and the empty-eyed.
And whether the upshot is a crown or drowning,
Each in his own way wades unreasonably;—

6.

Thirst is not reasoned. There is for each own darkness
No general compass. There is earned salt insight.
Only the birds don't earn, their resonance is free.

IV. More Than Wings Can Bear

1.

A leaf, a seagull falter.
What sudden pull is here?
Leaf, leaf on the water,
Gull, gull on the air:
Am I your overloader,
My side-glance your remolder?
Is even some age-old boulder
Outweighed by one brief stare?
   One wistful look at water
   Explodes your solid contour
   To nightmare's utmost border.
   Then back. To where?

2.

Fadings on the water.
Driftings on the air.
The inward and the outer,
Will and atom blur,
   Shaping a leaf-that-yellows
   To Aprils without shadows—
   And aimless wings to arrows
   That never were.

3.

Waif bob-bobbing on water.
Wisp fluffing on air.
Fantasy's flickering halter
Of gossamer
   Tugs—and a whole world's shimmer
   Obeys an eyelid's tremor.
   And sun, blind sun, seems dimmer
   Than inward flare.

4.

That symbol-making stare!
More weight than wings can bear.
More wing than wings can bear.
No shell can hold the meaning
That seeming gives to being;
Eon of overreaching,
Of trance that thirsts while feeding,
The story of man is there.
       Is there to fill and alter
       The leaf, leaf on the water,
       The seagull on the air.

v. Counter-Walk, Reversals

1.

The edge again, honed by a harder year
To rockbottom, harrowing all those low
Heights. Coming to terms with rock, the shadow
That soared shall walk. Enough scope walking. We're

Substance, grounded substance, and surprise
What warmth we can through all our outstretched senses:
Through skin the rub of skin, through ears and eyes
The goldfish-flicker of October branches.

The crayon of the sun pokes down and pencils—
The inkwell of the sea spills up and pens—
A crisscross of auroras on our brain-cells,
Which hurl back boomerangs of golden glance.

The fondling waves of years—for all their sweetness
Of breeze and brine—erode the body's dune.
Yet toward a craggy grace. Each ages toward concreteness.
Merely eternity is out of tune.

Somewhere a scale tilts earthward,
                              leaves the luring
Desert of spirit. Loam grows with ache and hazard
Our honest rat-death, no transcendent soaring.
And so we wrench a rose free from the desert.

The desert squeezes from a petal's palette
Attar, to hover permanent and pallid.
And leaves us dust to gnaw—I, dust heap, call it
Tang all the sweeter on my own doomed palate.

I, chunky gullet, curse whatever hovers.
My veins block the geometry of highways.
Guerilla of crooked and alluvial by-ways,
The sentenced heart stokes what palatial hovels.

Out. . . . Out. . . . An hourglass runs out,
The earth's and mine. A lamp, the sun's, goes out.
I, shivering sand pile, anyhow stretch out
Impossible warmth.
                    So lightning out of cloud.

Eye ear nose mouth and touch, the five surprisers—
For all their warmth—erode each aging face.
Wave after wave of horizontal geysers.
Yet toward a craggy grace.

2.*

Waste is the norm and grace the rarity,
One rose-red flicker in a ton of brambles.

* In triassic New England the characteristic mineral was its undry porous red
sandstone; the characteristic fauna were the dinosaurs and brontosaurs, dis-
tinguished not only by their size, but by their vertical third eyelid (nictitat-
ing membrane of lizards). Their footprints, surviving the intervening ice
age, are still found on New England sandstone today. The "Year" it takes
to condense sandstone from soil is capitalized as the year of a larger scale
than man's, as if coinciding with the so-called "Great Year" of the planet's
26,000-year equinoctial cycle.

I gambled half my life on aimless ambles,
Then stubbed against an aim,

      this crag by the sea.

What's rock but denser loam?—a weight of titans;
What's loam but looser rock?—New England coast;
According as the Year's accordion tightens
Or slackens

   in the sandstone holocaust.

New England sandstone: this triassic nettle,
Niched in the shagginess of unkempt earth,
Marking the line where leaf gives way to needle,
Old sentinel bisecting every north.

Such bulk cleaves more than merely firs from birches.
Sheer unabstractable substance rolls in vengeance
The past as avalanche; the future lurches;
The ice-age rolls upon the age of engines

A stony message: that there is no message.
To will what isn't or what is?—no passage
Between two halves of seeing,

     as if scissored
By nictitations of a thunder lizard.

Still vibrant from the trample of the saurians
Though drowsed of late beneath our pygmy tread,
Stone's layered eons warn the soul's historians
How truthful and how venerable is mud;

And just how brash is soul,

     not grace of rocks
But flutter-flutter Grace of Golden Treasury "pinions,"
Newfangled bootstrap of the simians,
An interloper meddling forth sermoned brooks:

Upholstering the emptiness of heaven,
Injecting emptiness in tomb and hearse,

The taxidermist of the universe. . . .
A scales reverses. Nothingness is heavy.

3.

Crossroads. My road tilts—where? Evade it? I,
Being both mud and air . . . does choose mean die?
But sullen winds are swelling from the sea.
And if I tilt no scales, the scales tilt me.

Then armed with vocatives shall I call rock "you"?
Invokings force a soul on you, O boulder.
Consciousness, just by being your beholder,
Demotes you to a symbol's retinue.

How many solstices and equinoxes
You've slept through, huddled seed in stolid eras—
Till annexationist man, unlocking boxes,
Walks by. Potentials quicken. Sleepers hear us:—

A droning, a terrible underground droning, the buried
Cicada hunger, dry wings flexing: burrowed
Abstraction, the late-born desert. Here to tame
This lithic balled fist of time.

Solidity hangs by a thread. When all's in deadlock,
Even a mote—by choosing—tips the balance.
Can I still sense, not shape, just sense your bedrock?
Or shall I choose to will with sculptor talons

Timeless mirage and with a sculptor's hatred
(Autumn and ebb and entropy undone)
Force meaning on you and hack unsatiated
Till stoniness is gutted out of stone?

Earth seems to offer us so gold an orchard
But locked in seeds, till hammered forth in torment.
And so with fruits of air, in dream-pods dormant.
Shall it not tempt that all be upward tortured—

By hammer, hammer, hammer—to almost sky?
When all's hallucinated what's one more lie?
It tempts, it tempts (that symbol-making stare).
RESIST. STAY STONE.
                    Well, we have got this far.